GAME SHOOTING

An Illustrated History

GAME SHOOTING

An Illustrated History

DAVID S D JONES

Quiller

Copyright © 2015 David S D Jones

First published in the UK in 2015
by Quiller, an imprint of Quiller Publishing Ltd

British Library Cataloguing-in-Publication Data
A catalogue record for this book
is available from the British Library

ISBN 978 1 84689 210 3

Book and jacket design by Sharyn Troughton
Printed in China

Quiller

An imprint of Quiller Publishing Ltd
Wykey House, Wykey, Shrewsbury, SY4 1JA
Tel: 01939 261616 Fax: 01939 261606
E-mail: info@quillerbooks.com
Website: www.quillerpublishing.com

CONTENTS

Comic shooting postcard 1905

Acknowledgements

FIRST, I MUST THANK THE MANY FRIENDS, acquaintances and professional colleagues in the world of game shooting and gamekeeping who have willingly supplied me with useful information for this book or have granted me access to archival material in their custody or possession. In particular, I would like to mention the following: Alastair Balmain; Clarissa Brown; Walter Cole; the late Don Ford; Sophia Gallia; Geoff Garrod; Ellie Glennie and James Hamilton of Abercorn Estates; Gillian Gooderham and Dr Mike Swan of the Game & Wildlife Conservation Trust; Jack Grasse; Marcus Janssen, editor of *Fieldsports*; David Kenyon; Lord Margadale; Brian Mitchell; Charles Nodder; Robert Philippi; Sarah Read; George Wallace; and Tim Weston.

Special thanks go to Mrs Georgina Rose for allowing me to quote from her book, *A Countrywoman's Year*. Thanks also to Keith McDougall for permitting me to use material from his privately published book of landscape paintings, *A Special Kind of Light*.

Various friends, contacts and professional organisations have willingly supplied me with photographs of game shooting activities, both past and present including: Abercorn Estates; Sir Andrew de la Rue, Bt.; the Game & Wildlife Conservation Trust; David Grass; Eddie Graves MBE; Hurworth Photography; Pete Jagger; Marcus Janssen; Andrew Johnston; David Mason; Sir Anthony Milbank, Bt.; Chris North; the late Captain John Rapley; Coenraad Vermaak Safaris; Lindsay Waddell; Barbara Whittle; and the West London Shooting School.

Finally, I would like to thank the many people whom I have met on the game fair circuit, in the sporting and farming community, and elsewhere over the past couple of decades who have supplied me with useful snippets of information relating to game shooting in times past or have pointed me in the direction of useful sources. Sadly, some did so without giving their names, but their help and advice is much appreciated.

Whilst every reasonable effort has been made to contact all copyright owners in whatever context, if I have omitted anyone or made any errors, I can only apologise and request that those affected contact the publishers in order that amends can be made in any subsequent printing of this edition.

David S.D. Jones

Summer 2015

Playing card advertising Schultze gunpowder 1910

Introduction

GAME SHOOTING
A BRIEF HISTORY

GAME SHOOTING FOR SPORTING PURPOSES has taken place in England and Wales since the reign of King Henry VIII in the first half of the sixteenth century. Using primitive matchlock and wheel lock guns to kill their quarry, the noblemen, soldiers and keepers of the royal hunting preserves of the day went

Georgian sportsman partridge shooting. Coloured engraving by C. Catton (after George Morland) 1789

out in pursuit of deer, wildfowl and game birds such as pheasants and partridges; shooting the birds while they were on the ground rather than in flight.

Realising the potential value of guns for warfare, King Henry VIII formed a firearms unit in his army in 1537. It was known as the Guild of St. George, and its soldiers were allowed to shoot not only at butts and marks but at all game and wildfowl. In 1542, King Henry introduced legislation regulating game shooting, restricting the privilege to his gamekeepers and foresters, and persons in possession of a Royal Licence who had an annual income of over £100. However, game shooting was considered to be 'un-sporting' by many of the aristocracy, who preferred falconry and hunting.

Sportsmen began to take a greater interest in game shooting during the Elizabethan period (1558–1603), especially after the introduction of the flintlock gun from the Continent towards the end of the sixteenth century. The sport was subsequently outlawed by King James I in 1603, when he made it a criminal offence to kill pheasants, partridges, grouse, wildfowl and other birds. Shooting suffered a further setback when Oliver Cromwell and his Puritan followers, who ruled Britain from 1649–1660, decided that game shooting, hunting and hawking were all 'frivolous amusements'.

The Restoration

King Charles II the first royal shot of note, who had spent many years living in exile in France, introduced the French practice of shooting at flying birds into England and Wales following the restoration of the monarchy in 1660. Keen to ensure that game shooting remained the privilege of the very rich, Charles passed an Act of Parliament in 1671 that restricted the right to kill game to landowners with a property worth over £100 a year, leaseholders in possession of land with an annual value of at least £150, their eldest sons and their authorised gamekeepers. He also allowed these men to shoot on land belonging to 'unqualified' persons such as impoverished squires and farmers, a move which proved to be very unpopular in the countryside.

The enthusiasm for game shooting continued to gather momentum during the late seventeenth and the early eighteenth centuries, and by 1750 shooting had become firmly established as a sport amongst the nobility and the wealthier landed gentry. Shooting became even more popular during the late eighteenth century and the first three decades of the nineteenth century following the introduction of the double-barrelled muzzle-loading gun and the invention of the percussion cap gun, a much more efficient weapon than the old flintlock gun. This enabled bigger bags of game. That said, early nineteenth century sportsmen generally carried on in a fairly leisurely manner, either going out alone or in small groups, accompanied by a gamekeeper and a couple of setters or pointers, walking-up and shooting partridges, pheasants and other birds. They rarely killed more game than they could eat.

Game shooting entered a new era in 1831 when King William IV passed a landmark Game Act which removed the property qualification for killing game, enabling any purchaser of a Game Certificate to go out in pursuit of game on a farm or estate provided that he had the owner's permission to do so. This legislation led to a massive increase in game shooting, game preservation, and gun ownership. It also established statutory shooting seasons for pheasants, partridges, grouse, hares and other types of game. Pheasants were actually still relatively scarce in many areas at this time, with partridges, grouse, hares and rabbits forming the principal quarry species pursued by sportsmen.

Battue or Driven Shooting

During the 1830s, some of the leading landowners of the day began to establish Continental-style *battue* or driven shoots on their properties. This method of shooting, which enabled a party of Guns to kill a large number of game birds within a short space of time, was further popularised by Prince Albert, the Prince Consort, who set up a driven shoot on the royal estate at Windsor in Berkshire shortly after his marriage to Queen Victoria in 1840.

Shooting changed yet again in the 1850s following the introduction of the breech-loading shotgun, which, like *battue*, gave a sportsman the opportunity to secure a big bag of game birds quickly and efficiently. Driven shooting suddenly started to take over from walked-up shooting even on relatively small estates from the 1860s onwards. Landowners began to artificially rear large

Battue *shooting in Lancashire. Coloured aquatint by T.J. Rawlins 1837*

numbers of pheasants in preference to preserving partridges, which were considered by many Victorian sportsmen to be less suitable for driven shooting. Big bags had now become the order of the day.

The Royal Example

Encouraged by Prince Edward, Prince of Wales (later to be King Edward VII), who had followed in his father's footsteps as a keen shot, young men of fashion took up shooting in preference to fox hunting – considered at the time to be a superior sport by many of the 'old aristocracy'. In 1862, the Prince, who had developed a passion for driven shooting by his teens and began shooting and deer stalking at an early age on the royal estates of Windsor and Balmoral, purchased the 8,000 acre Sandringham estate in Norfolk from the Honourable Spencer Cowper for the sum of £220,000 in order to have a sporting property where he could entertain his friends privately. Over the next ten years he spent almost £300,000 creating a 'state-of-the-art' shoot on the estate, guided by the Earl of Leicester, one of the leading shots of the day.

Throughout the late 1860s and the 1870s, Edward, Prince of Wales actively promoted driven pheasant and partridge shooting amongst the upper echelons of society, firmly establishing shooting as the leading field sport of the day in Great Britain. Indeed, through his influence shooting became a vitally important fixture on the social calendar along with Goodwood, Cowes Week and the London Season.

Prince Edward, Prince of Wales c. 1862

The Big Shot Era

The sport of driven game shooting undoubtedly reached its peak in the years between 1880 and 1914 – often referred to as the 'Big Shot era'. Shooting, however, was very much a minority activity at this time, limited to those who had the time and money to travel from one great house to another during the sporting season in order to kill large bags of game birds with an almost religious zeal. Some sportsmen, in fact, made a career out of shooting, spending the entire year in pursuit of game and travelling abroad to kill big game in Africa or India at the end of each season.

A group of smartly dressed Guns outside a country house c. 1890.
Note the different styles of shooting suit

*Edwardian partridge shooting party posing for the camera at Holdgate,
Shropshire, September 1903*

Sadly, the outbreak of World War One in 1914 signalled the end of shooting in the grand Edwardian manner. Sportsmen and gamekeepers serving in the Territorial Army immediately joined their units. Others followed suit, enlisting as volunteers in the army or the navy. Shooting activities were drastically reduced on estates everywhere, although pheasant rearing continued on some properties until 1917 when it became a criminal offence under the terms of the Defence of the Realm Act

Advertisement for Eley cartridges 1911

to feed grain and other foodstuffs to game birds. Few shoots were to survive the war years unscathed, all suffering from a lack of gamekeeping, deforestation, excessive poaching or temporary military occupation.

Shoots throughout the country were gradually revitalised in the aftermath of the war, albeit generally on a smaller scale than before, due to the burden of high taxation imposed upon landowners by the government. Some of the larger estates, owned by royalty, senior members of the aristocracy or extremely wealthy businessmen, continued to operate lavish Edwardian-style driven shoots. However, many smaller properties reverted to walked-up shooting with only a handful of big driven days being held during the course of the season.

HRH Prince Henry, Duke of Gloucester shooting on the Earl of Pembroke's estate at Wilton, Wiltshire 1920

Small shooting party at an unknown West Country location 1927

World War Two and Beyond

Game shooting continued to be carried out on a limited scale during World War Two, which lasted from 1939 until 1945, primarily for food procurement and vermin control rather than for sport. Thereafter, in the immediate post-war period, a combination of heavy poaching and a ban on artificial game bird rearing imposed during the war years, followed by rearing restrictions which lasted until the mid-1950s, caused game bird shortages that prevented landowners from rebuilding shoots for well over a decade.

Since the late 1950s, game shooting has changed beyond all recognition. Many well-known country house shoots have been redeveloped and are now operated along commercial or semi-commercial lines for the benefit of paying Guns. Superlative driven commercial shoots have been created from scratch in areas such as Exmoor and West Wiltshire, some of which specialise in providing high pheasants for discerning 'top end' sportsmen. Numerous small shoots have been started by syndicates of professional men who employ their own gamekeeping staff or by self-keepering syndicates whose members are more than happy to run their own shoot on a DIY basis. Shooting is, indeed, now more popular than ever, with men and women from all walks of life actively participating in the sport.

Shooting party at Stowell Park, Gloucestershire 2008: courtesy of Eddy Graves MBE.
Guns (left to right): Lord Vestey, Captain Peto, David Ker, the Hon. William Vestey,
Rhydian Morgan-Jones, the Hon. Mark Vestey, Brigadier Andrew Parker-Bowles,
the Hon. Arthur Vestey. Head keeper, Eddy Graves MBE is standing on
the far right of the photograph

TYPES OF
SHOOTING

OVER THE PAST THREE AND A HALF CENTURIES shooting has evolved from a minority sport, the strict preserve of the aristocracy and the landed gentry, to a social activity enjoyed by men and women from all walks of life. Shooting falls into two basic categories – walked-up and *battue*. It is usually carried out privately by a landowner, a sporting tenant or an organised syndicate of Guns. They might also operate on a semi-commercial or a commercial footing, letting out days to paying Guns, either individual or corporate.

Going out shooting. Coloured aquatint by T. Sutherland (after Dean Wolstenholme) 1823

Walked-up Shooting

Since the late seventeenth century, when the practice of shooting at flying birds rather than at birds standing on the ground was introduced into Great Britain from the Continent, sportsmen simply walked-up and shot pheasants, partridges and other game, using pointers, setters, Labradors, spaniels and other suitable dogs to flush out and to retrieve the quarry. Traditionally, sportsmen went out alone or in groups of two or three in the company of a gamekeeper, often spending the whole day trudging through the woods and fields or over the moors in order to shoot a few birds for the table. Later, walked-up shooting became more competitive, with Regency and early Victorian Guns vying with each other in order to see who could achieve the biggest bag of partridges, pheasants or grouse. Typical daily bags taken in Hampshire at this time by the

Sportsmen walking-up and shooting partridges over dogs. Coloured aquatint by H. Alken 1820

WALKED-UP SHOOTING AT AUDLEY END IN 1860

The 4th Lord Brayebrooke, a devotee of walked-up shooting, went out shooting on his estate at Audley End in Essex on a total of eighty-two days between 1 September 1860 and 1 February 1861, mainly accompanied by a gamekeeper. His game register for the season, which includes his own personal bag and a couple of combined bags from a few 'big days', records that he and his companions accounted for just over 4,000 head of game, comprising 723 pheasants, 925 partridges, 1,568 hares, 791 rabbits, 4 woodcock, 10 snipe, 42 wild duck, 1 teal and 3 landrail. Interestingly, the bag taken on an eight Gun day held at Audley End on 21 November 1860 amounted to a rather modest 81 partridges, 141 hares, 28 rabbits and 1 woodcock.

sporting diarist, Colonel Peter Hawker, included thirty-six partridges and one hare on 16 September 1816; eleven pheasants, three partridges and one hare on 1 October 1817; thirty-four partridges on 1 September 1830; and twenty-nine partridges and two hares on 3 September 1845.

Even after driven game shooting became the preferred method of shooting during the mid-Victorian period, walked-up shooting continued to be favoured on some smaller estates and on remote grouse moors which did not lend themselves to driving or were lightly preserved with relatively low stocks of birds. Walked-up days remained popular with a number of the more traditional landowners too. In addition to organising one or two driven shoots during the course of the season, they liked to spend a day or so out in the field every week in the company of a couple of old friends or a gamekeeper, and were not concerned about the size of the bag.

Following the outbreak of World War One, when landowners were obliged to scale down or abandon driven shooting operations due to staff shortages, walked-up shooting came into its own once again, not only providing sport for elderly Guns and off-duty servicemen, but also a means of procuring food for hospitals, convalescent homes and military training establishments. In the aftermath of the war, some estates, particularly those that had become impoverished by high taxation or death duties, substituted walked-up shooting

Farmers on a walked-up shoot in Dorset c. 1930

for driven shooting or even dispensed with their gamekeeping team altogether and operated an un-keepered rough shoot, shooting cock pheasants and partridges and the occasional hen bird, pigeons, ground game and whatever else was around.

Throughout the inter-war years, walked-up shooting continued to be carried out on a regular basis on a significant number of estates, with driven days being held on a much smaller scale that in the past. Thereafter, walked-up shooting predominated on the great majority of sporting properties for the next two decades after a government ban on artificial game bird rearing was imposed for the duration of the war years was followed by rearing restrictions which lasted from 1945 until the mid-1950s. In fact, driven shooting at this time became the sole preserve of a small number of ultra-rich landowners who could afford to employ a big enough team of gamekeepers to maintain sufficient stocks of pheasants and partridges through nest management and efficient vermin control, and those who owned large grouse moors.

The interest in walked-up shooting has increased dramatically since the late 1950s, despite the rapid growth in commercial and syndicate driven shooting during this period. Indeed, this method of shooting is extremely popular with all manner of sportsmen, ranging from wealthy paying Guns who prefer an enjoyable 'outside day' in the field in preference to the hustle and bustle of a high class driven shoot to those of limited means who belong to a self-keepering syndicate shoot or simply rent a block of rough shooting from a farmer or an estate and are content with a small but diverse bag.

Boundary Shooting

This is a form of walked-up shooting carried out in order to move pheasants and other game birds away from the boundary of an estate, from an outlying portion of an estate or from a less intensively shot area into the principal shooting grounds. Traditionally carried out from mid-November onwards by members of the gamekeeping team on an estate or by a landowner and one or two guests, boundary shooting has become increasingly attractive to paying Guns in recent years, particularly those on a limited budget or who want to enjoy a relaxing day in the field and are content with a small bag. On some commercial shoots, this activity is reserved for beaters, pickers-up and others involved with the shoot, as a reward for their help during the season.

Battue or Driven Shooting

Battue, the traditional name for driven game shooting, was first practised in central Europe during the early eighteenth century in order to enable wealthy noblemen to shoot a large head of game in one day. In the days leading up to the *battue*, peasants with dogs and nets would drive game into a wood from a large tract of the surrounding land. They would then encircle the wood with high netting. On the day of the *battue*, a group of peasants acting as beaters would enter the wood and drive the game out over the Guns. Sometimes as many as twenty-five men would participate in the event, each having at least six guns as well as their own team of loaders.

Surviving records for a large-scale *battue* shoot that took place over an eighteen-day period in September 1758 in Bohemia on an estate belonging to

Sportsman and beater out boundary shooting c. 1930

Prince Colloredo give an idea of the enormity of these events. In all, a party of forty-five Guns headed by the Emperor Francis I shot a total bag of 29,545 partridges, 9,004 pheasants, 3,320 snipe, 746 field larks, 13,243 hares, 1,710 wild boar, 3,216 deer, 932 foxes and 630 various. Some 300 gamekeepers were involved, assisted by 800 porters and around 1,750 beaters who had been recruited from nineteen villages.

Central European countries

Although wealthy British sportsmen travelled to Central European countries such as Austria, Bohemia and Hungary from time to time to participate in *battues* as invited guests of important noblemen, the sport of driven game shooting did not reach this country until the early nineteenth century. Even then it was slow to take off, not only due to the large expense involved in setting up and running a shoot of this kind, but because many landowners considered that the indiscriminate slaughter of large numbers of game birds was a barbaric and vulgar practice.

By the 1820s, driven shooting had started to take place on a regular basis on a few well-known English estates, including Knowsley in Lancashire, where a total of 27,000 head of game were killed by this method in 1825, and at Eaton Hall in Cheshire, where the 1st Marquess of Westminster was already artificially rearing pheasants to bolster up rapidly dwindling stocks of wild birds. The largest bag taken on a *battue* at this time, shot over a three-day period at Ashridge Park in Hertfordshire in January 1822, amounted to 1,200 head of game.

A minority sport

Driven shooting remained a minority sport until 1840 when Queen Victoria married Prince Albert of Saxe Coburg and Gotha. The Prince, a keen sportsman who was used to the large-scale shoots held in his German homeland, immediately set about popularising the *battue* in his adopted country and turned the royal estate at Windsor into a massive game preserve suitable for

Commencement of a battue *at Penwortham Hall, Lancashire. Coloured aquatint by T.J. Rawlins 1837*

entertaining important guests. This involved planting woods and coverts, rearing pheasants, putting down imported live hares, and acquiring additional sporting rights over nearby Bagshot Park.

Wealthy sportsmen, particularly younger men, soon began to follow the royal example, establishing driven shoots often in the hope of attracting Prince Albert and winning a coveted invitation to shoot at Windsor. By the mid-1840s the Prince was regularly visiting English estates to shoot pheasants in late autumn after returning from his annual deer stalking expedition in Scotland. In 1846, while staying with the Marquess of Salisbury at Hatfield in Hertfordshire, he created a new record on a *battue* by killing 150 head of game in 150 minutes, shooting with four guns.

The introduction of the breech-loading shotgun

The introduction of the breech-loading shotgun in the mid-1850s gave another boost to driven shooting. Many of the more traditional sportsmen who espoused walked-up shooting now switched to the driven method and started to artificially rear pheasants and plant game-friendly woods and coverts.

Over the next two decades, Prince Edward, Prince of Wales, the eldest son of Queen Victoria and Prince Albert, actively promoted driven shooting amongst the elite of society, particularly after he had purchased the Sandringham estate in Norfolk in order to pursue his interest in the sport. Within a very short space

Mid-Victorian sportsman with double-barrelled breech-loading shotgun

SHOOTING REPORT

We have been favoured with the following note of the shooting on the Earl of Stamford and Warrington's preserves at Bradgate, near Leicester, which began on the 10th and ended on the 14th, five days. First day – 3,333 rabbits, 8 pheasants, 12 wild duck, 3 woodcock, 3 snipe; total 3,359; number of Guns, 13. Second day – 173 hares, 190 rabbits, 1,605 pheasants, 26 woodcock, 3 various; total, 1,997; number of Guns, 14. Third day – 193 hares, 267 rabbits, 736 pheasants, 7 woodcock, 3 various; total, 1,206; number of Guns, 13. Fourth day – 61 hares, 245 rabbits, 1 partridge, 1,185 pheasants, 12 woodcock, 1 snipe, 9 various; total, 1,514; number of Guns, 13. Fifth day – 55 hares, 257 rabbits, 75 pheasants, 2 wild duck, 10 woodcock, 1 various; total, 400; number of Guns, 5. Grand total, 8,476 head. Nearly all of this enormous quantity of game was distributed amongst the tenantry and poor of the district.

The Inverness Courier 26 December 1861

of time shooting took priority over agriculture in many parts of the British Isles. Large numbers of gamekeepers were recruited to rear pheasants and partridges, foresters were employed to manage areas of woodland, and armies of farm workers were given the chance to earn extra money as beaters on shoot days.

By 1875, driven shooting had become firmly established as the leading field sport, not only throughout much of England and Wales but also on many Scottish and Irish estates. Virtually every major landowner, both aristocratic and newly rich businessman was now striving to build up a shoot that could provide daily bags of between 500 and 1,000 pheasants, usually in the hope of attracting top shots such as the Marquess of Ripon, Lord Walsingham, the Maharaja Duleep Singh or even Edward, Prince of Wales.

An important social fixture

Throughout the late Victorian and Edwardian periods, driven shooting was an important fixture on the social calendar on most large estates during the autumn and winter months. Edward, Prince of Wales, who ascended the throne as King Edward VII in 1902, dominated the world of shooting at this time, and made an

Royal shooting party at Chatsworth, 3 January 1907. Guns standing in the front row include King Edward VII (fourth from left) and the celebrated shot, the 2nd Marquess of Ripon (third from left). On one drive alone, the Marquess of Ripon bagged a total of 184 pheasants, 26 wild duck and over 30 hares

annual 'progress' around top shoots such as Chatsworth, Eaton, Elveden and Holkham right up until the time of his death in 1910.

Driven shooting continued to take place on a grand scale until the outbreak of World War One in 1914. In fact, in the last full season before the war, a party of seven Guns headed by King George V took an all-time record bag of 3,937 pheasants at a *battue* held on 18 December 1913 at Hall Barn in Buckinghamshire, seat of Lord Burnham, the then proprietor of the *Daily Telegraph*. This event has been described as the high point of the 'Big Shot' era.

World War One and beyond

Sadly, punitive taxation imposed by the Lloyd George Liberal Government following the cessation of hostilities in 1918 meant that many of the top driven shoots in Great Britain were not only obliged to make drastic economies in order to survive but in some cases needed to 'recruit' the odd paying Gun in order to defray part of the management costs, or to lease the shooting rights over some of the beats to private or syndicate sporting tenants. However, a few of the great shoots, owned by the Duke of Westminster, the Duke of

Rutland and a few other wealthy landowners continued to operate along Edwardian lines until the declaration of World War Two in 1939, when shooting for sporting purposes excluding small-scale walked-up or driven shooting for food procurement and vermin control was discontinued for the duration of the war on virtually every estate in the land.

Game bird rearing restrictions enacted by the Labour Government in the wake of World War Two prevented landowners and private or syndicate tenants from re-building driven shoots until the mid-1950s, when economic constraints, in particular high labour costs, necessitated the introduction of 'let days' on many estates. Today, the great majority of driven shoots are run along commercial or semi-commercial lines and provide shooting facilities for paying Guns, both private and corporate.

Syndicate Shooting

Although seen by many as a product of the late 1950s and the 1960s, syndicate shooting actually began in the mid-Victorian period when groups of newly rich

The Callow Syndicate, Leigh Hall, Shropshire – relaxed, convivial and enjoying every moment of the day: courtesy of Andrew Johnston

but landless businessmen started to rent the sporting rights over small estates or large owner-occupied farms within easy reach of towns and cities. Keen to have a shoot of their own, these men, many of whom were good shots having served as non-commissioned officers in territorial regiments, worked hard to create small walked-up shoots, but often suffered at the hands of a hostile gamekeeper keeping a 'watching brief' on behalf of the landowner. They were also looked down upon by the aristocracy and the landed gentry and were unlikely to be asked to demonstrate their prowess as a guest at a 'society' shooting party.

Syndicate tenancies on Scottish estates

The Scottish sporting letting system, however, another Victorian innovation, enabled wealthy businessmen and professionals, particularly those who had prospered on the Stock Exchange, in the law or in the railway and brewing industries, to form syndicates to rent or lease mixed shooting and fishing estates or small deer forests in the Highlands and Islands, where the members could retreat during late summer and early autumn on a 'timeshare' type basis. Such shooting syndicates were treated on an equal footing along with the more traditional sporting tenants by members of the Scottish landowning fraternity, so long as they were able to pay their rental fees, and many lasted well into the Edwardian era.

Sportsmen on a Scottish grouse moor c. 1910. Syndicates of businessmen and professionals regularly rented Scottish sporting properties throughout the late Victorian and the Edwardian periods

The concept of the shooting syndicate in England South of the border, the concept of the shooting syndicate started to become more socially acceptable, with groups of London businessmen renting shoots in the Home Counties and the more accessible parts of East Anglia which could be reached by train within an hour or two. Syndicate shooting in these regions gradually increased until the outbreak of World War One, when shoots were either mothballed or scaled down for the duration.

Peter and Thirza Grass, head gamekeeper and housekeeper to Lord Noel-Buxton's East Hall shooting syndicate: courtesy of David Grass

In the aftermath of the war, many landowners who had been hit by the high taxation imposed by the Lloyd George Government, or by death duties, saw the financial benefits that could be gained from letting out the shooting rights over part of their property to syndicates of wealthy businessmen, irrespective of their social status, and took active steps to secure sporting tenants. Indeed, the ultra-rich Earl of Iveagh, owner of the celebrated Elveden estate in Suffolk, leased a 5,000 acre section of his shoot to a syndicate of seven Guns, while the Earl of Pembroke divided up the 50,000 acre Wilton estate in Wiltshire into three shoots, letting two to separate syndicates and retaining the third, a mere 6,000 acres for himself.

Further, it was not uncommon during this period for groups of businessmen to purchase estates at bargain prices in order to secure the shooting rights. For example, in 1930, a syndicate of businessmen headed by the Labour peer Lord Noel-Buxton, acquired the 3,000 acre East Hall estate at Feltwell in Norfolk, ancestral seat of the Upcher family, in order to obtain a first-rate partridge shoot. In keeping with his socialist beliefs, Lord Noel-Buxton invited the head keeper, Peter Grass, to move into the hall on the condition that he and his wife would provide overnight accommodation for syndicate members and their guests during the shooting season.

Grouse moor syndicates

By the early 1930s, according to various contemporary accounts, a large number of top Yorkshire grouse moors had been leased to syndicates of stockbrokers, manufacturers and other wealthy businessmen by the impoverished owners in order that they could keep their property for future generations. Not content with a traditional moorland shooting lodge, these Guns usually took a suite of rooms in a luxurious hotel in Harrogate or another convenient town, travelling daily to the moor by chauffeur driven Rolls-Royce.

It goes without saying, of course, that many of these syndicates viewed shooting along business lines rather than in sporting terms, even to the extent of charging individual members per brace of pheasants or partridges taken – at the rate paid by the local game dealer. Syndicate shoots at this time were not entirely popular with members of the fox hunting fraternity either, as some pursued an active 'anti fox' policy, instructing the keeping staff to kill all foxes to prevent game losses.

World War Two

Syndicate shooting continued to operate on a limited scale throughout World War Two from 1939 to 1945, with walked-up shooting being substituted for driven shooting and places being given to off-duty servicemen on many shoots in order to make up numbers. Thereafter, the syndicate system of shooting really began to take off in the late 1940s and the 1950s, with groups of Guns from the professional and business classes renting the sporting rights from farmers and other landowners (some of whom acquired a Gun in the syndicate as part of the deal) and employing their own gamekeeper to manage the shoot, as well as recruiting beaters, dog handlers and other support staff. Some with long term leases even built their own luncheon hut at a convenient point on the shoot.

In the late 1950s, the owners of a number of the more prestigious English country house shoots took advantage of the syndicate system, forming small private syndicates of paying Guns as a means of defraying operating costs, allocating a specific number of places to these Guns at each shooting party. Earl Mountbatten of Burma, for example, proprietor of the Broadlands estate in Hampshire, set up the Broadlands Syndicate for this purpose, retaining three Guns for himself and his guests and selling the remaining five to Sir Thomas and Lady Sopwith, Mr C. G. Clover and other 'blue chip' clients.

The advent of the self-keepering syndicate

The early 1960s saw the advent of the self-keepering syndicate, which enabled Guns of limited means to rent the shooting rights over a small area of land from a farmer, an estate or a public body such as the Forestry Commission, and to run a shoot on a DIY basis at a minimal cost. This system brought shooting within reach of enthusiastic factory workers, office staff and others, all of whom were prepared to work hard in their spare time rearing their own pheasants, controlling vermin, etc. in order to have their own walked-up or driven shoot.

From the mid-1960s onwards, the syndicate started to dominate the world of driven game shooting, fuelled by the willingness of many of the more traditional landowners to lease a high quality shoot either in part or in its entirety to an organised group of Guns, who not infrequently paid all of the gamekeeping costs, too. Indeed, even with the rapid growth in commercial shooting since the 1980s, syndicate shooting continues to be popular with Guns who can afford to maintain their own private shoot, some of whom let spare days to offset management costs.

Game records for the East Farm syndicate shoot at Fovant Wiltshire 1948; a typical small farmers' shoot: courtesy of Fovant History Interest Group

A group of farmer-sportsmen in Hampshire 1979: courtesy of the GWCT. Shooting syndicates have long been popular amongst members of the farming community

The 'roving' or 'roaming' syndicate

In recent years, syndicate shooting has evolved yet again, with the development of the 'roving' or 'roaming' syndicate – a group of Guns who pay to shoot in a number of different locations throughout the country, not only on prestigious pheasant and partridge shoots but on top grouse moors too. Such syndicates are more often than not organised by sporting agents, who have the necessary expertise and contacts to offer the widest range of challenging shooting opportunities.

Syndicate shooting has undoubtedly been the saviour of driven game shooting in the United Kingdom over the past ninety years or so, ensuring the survival of a great many traditional country house shoots and bringing game shooting within easy reach of folk from all walks of life, making shooting a democratic rather than an exclusive sport.

Commercial Shooting

Shooting along commercial lines first began in a small way in the 1920s when impoverished landowners started to take in one or two paying Guns on driven shoots in order to offset some of their operating costs. Usually newly rich businessmen who were keen to rub shoulders with members of the landed gentry or impoverished aristocrats, such Guns were discreetly 'recruited' through a sporting agent, a solicitor or other intermediary and were equally as keen as their host not to disclose that any financial transaction had taken place.

Commercial shooting, however, continued to be a relatively low-key affair until the mid-1970s when a number of enterprising landowners and businessmen saw the potential of creating high quality shoots, modelled along private estate shoot lines, specifically for the benefit of paying Guns, in particular those who did not wish to be tied down to the same shoot or to commit themselves to membership of a shooting syndicate.

For example, in 1973, David Hitchens a successful Wiltshire farmer opened what is now the internationally famous Gurston Down shoot near Salisbury, concentrating specifically on providing high pheasants for wealthy paying Guns. Several shoot owners in the south-west of England subsequently followed in his footsteps, creating commercial high pheasant shoots on Exmoor, most notably Milton's, Molland and Castle Hill, despite Exmoor not being a landscape entirely suited to holding game birds. Landowners in other parts of the country gradually jumped on the bandwagon during the late 1970s and the early 1980s, setting up commercial shoots for a growing clientele.

Some titled landowners with old established shoots followed suit, converting from private to semi-commercial or wholly commercial operations, letting out driven pheasant and partridge days to paying guests in order to derive an additional income from their estates. The more enterprising amongst them offered clients a selection of value-added packages ranging from dinner with the duke to dinner, bed and breakfast in a stately home, options particularly popular with Guns from the United States.

Over the past thirty years or so, commercial shoots have gone from strength to strength, attracting not only individual paying Guns or parties of paying Guns, both from home and abroad, but also corporate customers who buy shoot days to entertain clients or to reward staff. Indeed, a significant number of driven pheasant and partridge shoots in the United Kingdom are now run along commercial lines. Many of the smaller walked-up pheasant shoots are also operated on a business footing, letting out days to private clients in order to help defray some of the running costs.

Shooting high pheasants at Gurston Down, Wiltshire, January 1983: courtesy of the GWCT

THE
SHOOTING DAY

THE SUCCESS OF A SHOOTING DAY depends not only upon the weather, the company, the quality of the hospitality and the size and variety of the bag, but also on the hard work carried out beforehand by the host, the gamekeeping staff and others connected with the shoot. Comfortable and waterproof clothing and footwear can contribute to the enjoyment of the day too, especially if shooting in cold winter weather or over rough terrain, as can the provision of suitable vehicles for transport between drives or beats and, if necessary, for shelter in the event of a sudden downpour. Last, but not least, the satisfaction of going home with a brace of birds for the table and entering details of the day's activities in one's game book for posterity can add the final touch to a memorable day in the field.

Guns and their ladies in a jocular mood at the start of a shooting day on the Hatherop estate, Gloucestershire 1905

Archibald Weyland Ruggles-Brise recalls some details of the shooting day programme at Spains Hall in Essex during the mid-Victorian period in *Shooting Reminiscences in Essex and Elsewhere* published in 1936:

'To go back to early days in my home, 1850–60, as a child, I remember an army arriving overnight, consisting of guests, valets, loaders, coachmen, pairs of horses, dogs. Where they all got to I did not inquire, nor do I know now, but all turned up spick and span the next morning, ready by 10.30 a.m. Shooting did not commence until 11 a.m. The Guns, after a brandy and soda or a beer, proceeded to the rendezvous, where the keeper had everything in readiness. But we must bear in mind that unless the woods and coverts were in a hilly country the pheasants were not so much thought about as now, and many more pheasants were killed inside the woods in the rides, also a very large amount of ground game. The game was all sent home and laid out on the front lawn, ready for the Guns to inspect on their arrival home.'

ELVEDEN SHOOTING.

Arrangements for _____

CARS leave Elveden Hall _____ a.m.

MEET at _____ a.m.

AMMUNITION VAN to start from the Hall _____ a.m.

CONVEYANCE for LOADERS   ditto _____ a.m.

LUNCHEON at _____ at _____ p.m.

N.B.—It is particularly requested that all KEEPERS and LOADERS be ready to start at _____ a.m., ELVEDEN TIME.

Head Keeper.

Shooting day programme card for the Elveden estate, Suffolk c. 1920. The clocks at Elveden were advanced half-an-hour during the shooting season to enable the day's proceedings to start early and to finish in late afternoon before the light had completely gone

Shoot Meals and Hospitality

Considered to be an essential part of the shooting day programme at the present time, shoot meals have, nevertheless, been around since the latter part of the eighteenth century when the sportsmen of the day, who often shot from early morning to late afternoon, carried a sandwich or two in a specially made case and a flask of brandy for refreshment purposes. Meals continued to be fairly Spartan until the early Victorian period when shooting became much more of a social activity and the rapidly growing railway network enabled landowners to hold residential shooting house parties, inviting friends from distant parts to come and stay for a long weekend or a week or more at a time. By the Edwardian era, the shooting party had become an established institution during the autumn and winter months with members of the royal family, the aristocracy and the landed gentry progressing from one country house to another, enjoying luxurious accommodation, fine dining, superlative shooting by day, and card

Shooting party at Windsor Castle on the occasion of the German Kaiser's visit, November 1907. Guns standing in the back row include the King of Spain (far left), the Kaiser (second from left) and King Edward VII (far right)

games in the evening. Hospitality of this kind eventually became unaffordable and was either superseded by the country house shooting weekend or disbanded entirely in favour of non-residential shoot days. Today, shoot accommodation, if required, is generally provided in purpose-built shooting lodges, some of which also have dining rooms, while lunch is usually taken in a dedicated luncheon room, a lodge dining room or in a nearby hotel or public house.

Breakfast

Victorian and Edwardian sportsmen invariably enjoyed a substantial cooked breakfast prior to spending a day out on the shooting field. Served in the dining room of a country house at a relatively early hour, the fare on offer normally included eggs and bacon, ham, kidneys, kedgeree, kippers and other fish dishes with, perhaps, game pie and grilled pheasant or partridge. On smaller, non-residential shoots at this time, breakfast might be taken in a farmhouse or a gamekeeper's cottage, the food being provided by the host and cooked by the farmer's or the keeper's wife. Later, on non-residential shoots, breakfast frequently became the responsibility of the individual Gun who either snatched a bite to eat before he left home or stopped off at a public house or café for eggs and bacon or similar en-route to his destination.

In recent years, it has become something of a tradition, particularly on commercial and syndicate shoots, to serve breakfast in a shoot luncheon room not only so that Guns can get to know each other, if strangers, but in order that the host or designated shoot captain can meet and greet everyone in a relaxed atmosphere, discuss the plans for the day and give a short safety talk. Modern-day shoot breakfast fare can range from coffee and home-made biscuits or hot sausage rolls to a full fry-up with toast and marmalade, washed down with a large mug of tea.

Elevenses

Usually taken after the second drive, the mid-morning break or elevenses stop is considered to be an essential part of the modern shooting day. Refreshments offered can vary tremendously from shoot to shoot but typically include coffee, sloe gin, sherry or bullshot (a mixture of vodka and beef consommé served very

Sportsmen enjoying liquid elevenses at Grayrigg, Westmorland 1913

hot) with hot sausages, savoury biscuits and other snack items. It is not unusual for a large shoot to have a number of elevenses points, utilising old barns, follies or other buildings of interest for food service, for shelter in inclement weather, and to provide toilet facilities for the Guns.

In times past, when sportsmen often shot through until luncheon, elevenses were usually taken on the hoof and consisted of little more than a couple of biscuits or a sandwich washed down with part of the contents of a hip flask or a pint of beer. However, in exceptional circumstances, a substantial mid-morning feast might be served in the open air after the second drive had concluded as Lord Dorchester experienced in 1901 at a shoot hosted by a newly ennobled politician to celebrate his elevation to the peerage. He recounts: 'We adjourned to a group of tables where liveried attendants restored our exhausted frames with every kind of liqueur, besides the appropriate sandwiches, pate de fois, caviar, etc.'

Lunch

One of the highlights of the modern shooting day, especially on commercial shoots, is lunch. The concept of organising a formal shoot lunch dates back to the early Victorian period when Queen Victoria's husband, Albert, the Prince Consort, began to promote driven game shooting and introduced the custom of having a hot luncheon at three in the afternoon, after shooting had concluded for the day. Prior to this time, sportsmen, who were generally more interested in shooting than eating a sumptuous lunch, simply made their own sandwiches at the breakfast table, using cold meat, eggs or whatever else was available.

Hot after-shoot lunches soon became the order of the day on the great majority of sporting properties, and continued to be held at 3 p.m. until King Edward VII succeeded Queen Victoria in 1901 and introduced the practice of having a lunch break at around 1 p.m. so that shooting could continue until late afternoon. Lunches on top shoots often consisted of three or more courses, with luxury food on the menu and a choice of fine wines and liqueurs, plus a selection of cigars. On some estates, it was the practice for the head gamekeeper to enter the dining room before lunch was completely over and to announce the morning's bag to the assembled company, which also acted as a signal for the Guns to prepare to depart for the first drive of the afternoon.

Shoot lunch – German style c. 1910

Shoot lunches during late Victorian and Edwardian times were usually taken in the main house on a country estate, in a specially built luncheon lodge (or a shooting box on a grouse moor), in a gamekeeper's house or in a farmhouse. Some landowners however, preferred to use the German system of eating a substantial cooked lunch off a fully laid-up table in a woodland glade, with a butler and a footman in attendance for service purposes.

Even then, a number of the more traditional country landowners chose to eat outside, dining on fairly basic fare, a practice continued at Sandringham for partridge shooting until the time of King George VI. The 2nd Viscount Portman, for example, owner of the Bryanston estate in Dorset and Master of the Portman Hunt from 1858 until his death in 1919, always lunched in a sheltered part of a wood or under the lee of a hayrick, providing his shooting guests with a communal brown paper parcel of sliced cold game or chicken, every man helping himself by digging his fork into the bit he fancied. For afters, each Gun was issued with a biscuit, a piece of cheese and a slice of cake.

Lunch break in a farmyard at Coln St.Aldwyn's, Gloucestershire 1904

Some shooting enthusiasts eschewed a hot lunch in favour of a cold meal, considering that the former had an effect on performance in the afternoon. Sir Ralph Payne-Gallwey, writing in *Letters to Young Shooters* in 1894, warned readers:

> 'A very heavy luncheon is very detrimental to straight shooting – even the difference between a hot midday meal and a cold one has an influence sometimes on the way birds come down to Guns in the late afternoon. I do not for a moment intend to convey that liquid refreshments are to be blamed – but a menu of puddings and pies and strong cigars, perhaps in a hot room in a farmhouse, are quite sufficient to put a shooter off his aim at any time.'

Lavish shoot lunches were disbanded on all but the wealthiest of estates following the outbreak of the Great War in 1914 due to a lack of guests, staff shortages and, in some instances, a lack of suitable food. In fact, until the cessation of hostilities in 1918, sandwiches or meat pies were the usual luncheon fare. If military guests were present, ration packs would be provided by the cookhouse at a local army camp.

Thereafter, from the 1920s until the 1970s, shoot lunches appear to have been a case of feast or famine dependent upon the whims of the host or the views of shooting syndicate members. Although some landowners continued the tradition of fine dining in a country house or a farmhouse, it was not uncommon during this period for sportsmen to bring their own lunch from home in a haversack or in a picnic parcel provided by the host and to eat the meal in a barn, under a hedge, in a wooden hut on a grouse moor or in the back of an old lorry!

Since the 1970s, however, the hot shoot lunch has enjoyed a renaissance on both private and commercially operated shoots, and is now an integral part of the shooting day package. Indeed, over the past thirty years or so many landowners and shoot operators have built special luncheon lodges or lodges that provide accommodation as well as dining facilities, or they have converted farm buildings into luncheon rooms in order that sportsmen can dine in comfort and style.

LUNCH UNDER CANVAS

Not content with dining in the specially built luncheon lodges which could be found at strategic locations on many great estates, or in dedicated rooms in gamekeepers' cottages or tenant farmhouses, affluent late Victorian and Edwardian sportsmen often owned a commodious marquee which could be erected on the field if shooting was taking place on a distant beat or over leased land. The 1st Earl of Iveagh, for example, possessed a deluxe marquee with a boarded floor, glass windows and heating facilities, which had a dining table capable of accommodating up to forty people. If the shooting party was several days' duration, this marquee would be put up at a different place on his 25,000 acre Elveden estate in Suffolk each day.

Shooting party posing for the camera outside the luncheon marquee at Sydenham House, Marystow, Devon 1914

Afternoon tea

Something of a shooting day tradition since the Edwardian era, when the custom of having a large after-shoot luncheon at 3 p.m. was disbanded in favour of an earlier lunch break in order that shooting could continue until late afternoon, afternoon tea can range from a simple snack consisting of a cup of tea and a piece of fruit cake in the luncheon lodge at the end of a commercial day to a substantial meal of toasted crumpets with jam or honey, sandwiches and home-made cakes in the hall of a country house, washed down with hot chocolate, Bovril or something stronger! Interestingly, on many of the Yorkshire grouse moors during the 1920s and '30s, afternoon tea was a pay-for affair, the Guns eating in a farm house on their way back from the moor to their shooting quarters. On Stean Moor, in Nidderdale, for example, Mrs Nowell of Moor House Farm charged the Guns 1/3d (6p) for a cup of tea, hot scones with jam and cake in her parlour but provided the loaders, who sat in the kitchen, with similar fare for 1/- (5p).

In addition to satisfying the inner man prior to departure for home, an afternoon tea break at the end of the day, be it short or long, provides a useful opportunity for a team of Guns to discuss the day's sport while the final pick-up is taking place, to exchange contact details if strangers, and to be present when the head gamekeeper or shoot manager announces the closing bag figure. On a residential shoot, tea time enables the Guns to relax with their ladies in front of the fire after a hard day out in the open and chat or read the daily paper prior to having a quick nap and a hot bath before dressing for dinner.

Overnight accommodation

Prior to the outbreak of the Great War in 1914, when shooting was an elite social sport confined to the aristocracy and the landed gentry, Guns and their wives or mistresses invariably stayed with their host in his castle or country house as part of a house party, either for a long weekend or for a whole week. If insufficient suitable accommodation was available in the main house for all of the guests at a big shoot, it was the custom to board young bachelor Guns in specially reserved rooms at the head keeper's cottage or in a local hotel. Valet-loaders and other personal attendants were billeted wherever their master happened to be staying. The house party arrangement continued to be popular

Welbeck Abbey, Nottinghamshire; seat of the 6th Duke of Portland and a regular venue for royal and aristocratic shooting house parties prior to the outbreak of the Great War in 1914

on the more prestigious sporting estates until the 1930s. Thereafter, ease of road and rail transport enabled guests to visit shoots on a daily basis, especially those who could no longer afford to sustain a life of total leisure and found that they needed to work for a living in the City or elsewhere during the week.

Lengthy shooting house parties were gradually superseded by country house weekends where guests arrived on a Friday night, shot on a Saturday, relaxed or went riding on a Sunday morning and departed in the afternoon. Popular with Guns who have a limited amount of spare time, such weekends continue to be hosted by many landowners for family members and friends.

Shooting became much more of a localised activity during the 1950s and '60s, with many people of limited means taking up the sport who were neither in a position to afford to travel very far or to pay for sleeping accommodation. In fact, by this time, even some of the wealthier sportsmen rarely travelled more than fifty or sixty miles to a shoot, unless they were going to visit a grouse moor.

However, the rapid growth in commercial shooting over the past thirty years

Bake Barn Shooting Lodge on the Fonthill estate, Wiltshire. Recently converted from agricultural buildings, the lodge can be easily reached from the A303 and is not only used for shoot purposes but is also available for hire for meetings and as a wedding venue

or so, particularly in the West Country, has created a new demand for dedicated overnight accommodation. Keen shots, some from as far afield as Europe and the United States, now require high quality but homely facilities, preferably in the company of fellow sportsmen, something not always available in hotels or public houses where guests might include a goodly complement of general holiday makers. Further, sportsmen, who until recently drove out from London to shoots in Wiltshire, Dorset or Somerset or in East Anglia on a daily basis, within the space of a couple of hours, are now finding they need somewhere to sleep over prior to a shoot day as congestion and regular hold-ups on routes such as the A303 and the A12 often prevent them from reaching their destination on time.

The comfortable lounge area at Bake Barn

Landowners and shoot proprietors have risen to this challenge, converting farmhouses or outbuildings such as 'character' barns into comfortable shooting lodges or, even, building new lodges. Many provide full-board overnight accommodation inclusive of dinner, bed and breakfast and have a games room and a small bar where guests can relax in the evening. Some can arrange shooting on a variety of estates and offer stalking and fishing facilities as well.

Shooting lodges, of course, come in all shapes and sizes and while some provide great accommodation in a homely environment and good, traditional English cooking, others are run along the lines of an old fashioned country house, offering the kind of facilities enjoyed by a country squire in times past, richly furnished rooms full of antiques and oil paintings, and fine dining with waitress and butler service. Crowcombe Court, for example, a former seat of the

Carew family set amidst the Quantock Hills in Somerset, operated both as a shooting lodge and a hunting box by the resident owners, David and Kate Kenyon, offers sporting guests a unique break in the elegant surroundings on a Georgian mansion. Fieldsports enthusiasts themselves, they not only arrange shooting on a variety of prestigious Exmoor estates but also provide a base from where it is possible to hunt six days a week, with a choice of thirteen different packs of foxhounds, staghounds, harriers and beagles!

SHOOTING BOXES

Commonly found in Yorkshire and other northern counties, where they were built to accommodate owners, tenants and lessees of grouse moors during the shooting season, large residential shooting boxes were occasionally erected in other parts of the country, too, for the same purpose.

Such 'low ground' shooting boxes were generally constructed by a landowner to house the shooting tenants of an outlying portion of a large estate or by a long term sporting lessee. Boxes invariably contained servants quarters and had a gamekeeper's cottage nearby.

North Creake shooting box, Norfolk. Built by Earl Spencer in the nineteenth century, the box was used as a hostel by the Women's Land Army during World War Two

Clothing and Accessories

Seen by many as a Victorian innovation, bespoke shooting clothing actually dates back to the mid-eighteenth century when, according to contemporary paintings, fashionable sportsmen dressed in a dark knee-length coat made of a green, blue, red or brown cloth, a white waistcoat, dark-coloured breeches, stockings and shoes and wore either a dark tricorn hat or a top hat. Prior to this time, both sportsmen and gamekeepers appear to have worn an identical attire consisting of a dark green coat and waistcoat, dark coloured breeches, stockings, shoes and a dark-coloured hat.

Sportsmen out in the field dressed in typical early nineteenth century shooting attire.
Coloured aquatint by C. Bentley (after H. Alken) 1835

Green and brown eventually seem to have become the preferred colours for shooting coats, as Thomas observed in his *Shooter's Guide*, published in 1820:

> 'Many sportsmen have carried the business of shooting to such a nicety as to be choice in the colour of dress. Green they have supposed to be the best in the early part of the season, and, when winter approaches, a kind of light brown, resembling stubble: this last colour, however, will be found to answer throughout the season.'

The sportsmen of the day, however, often chose to wear white, cream or light brown trousers or breeches on the shooting field which although stylish were unsuited for walking through undergrowth or across muddy terrain. While the more sensible amongst them wore brown leather leggings for calf and ankle protection, the great majority were quite happy to expose their leg-wear to the elements down to the top of their shoes.

Tweed suiting

Sportsmen continued to dress in what might be considered fashionable but not entirely practical clothing until the mid-nineteenth century. Thereafter, from the 1850s onwards, men became conscious of the need for comfortable clothing that was not only warm and waterproof but also allowed unrestricted movement when shooting and, if necessary, could act as camouflage on a grouse moor or in a deer forest. This resulted in the clothiers of the day designing and manufacturing shooting suits in a variety of styles and colours made from tweed sourced from Scotland and other parts of the United Kingdom. Tweed was recognised as a versatile material that was both thorn-proof and shower-proof. Tweed suiting, either hand-made or 'off the peg', soon became popular amongst members of the sporting fraternity, particularly those who paid an annual visit to Scotland for shooting, fishing and deer stalking. Indeed, some landowners even commissioned their own dedicated estate tweed for use by themselves, members of their family and their gamekeeping staff.

By the late Victorian period, the bespoke tweed shooting suit had become firmly established as the costume not only for fashionable sportsmen but also for gamekeepers and for loaders, many of whom wore an identical suit to their master. Usually consisting of a jacket, waistcoat and trousers (either 'plus two',

Shooting party on a Cheshire estate c. 1950. Sportsmen and gamekeepers are all wearing tweed suits, albeit in slightly varying styles

'plus four', or straight) or breeches, and often with a matching cloth cap or trilby-type hat, this attire has stood the test of time, styles having varied a little over the years according to prevalent fashions, and continues to be extremely popular today.

That said, many modern Guns now make do for less formal occasions with a combination of breeches (often referred to as 'breeks'), jersey and tweed shooting coat, fleece or shooting waistcoat and reserve their tweed suiting for use on 'big days' or on the grouse moor!

Footwear

Fashionable but functional footwear considered suitable for use with tweed suiting during the late Victorian and the Edwardian periods usually consisted of leather leggings and boots or woollen stockings, leather spats (short gaiters) and shooting shoes. From the 1920s onwards, woollen stockings and leather shoes became the preferred form of footwear both on low ground shoots and on the grouse moor. They continue to be fashionable at the present time, although some sportsmen now prefer to wear woollen stockings and rubber or leather shooting boots.

Head gear

Late nineteenth and early twentieth century sportsmen wore a variety of hats ranging from caps and trilby-type hats to bowler hats and deer stalkers. However, over the past century or so, the cloth cap, despite its working class associations, has become the most popular form of shooting headwear, being both practical and versatile. Some shooting enthusiasts, of course, eschew the cap in favour of wide-brimmed leather hats, American hunting caps, Glengarry hats and all manner of other flamboyant creations!

In addition to wearing a hat, many modern-day sportsmen take the sensible precaution of donning either a pair of earmuffs or earplugs in order to protect their hearing systems. Deafness caused by persistent shooting was something of an occupational hazard amongst shooters in times past.

Weatherproof outer clothing

If in need of protection against rain and wind, hardy Victorian and Edwardian sportsmen invariably wore a tweed cape or Ulster over their tweed shooting suit. This mode of apparel was replaced by the waterproof mackintosh or shooting coat manufactured by Burberry and other companies during the early years of the

Advertisement for the 'Mosco' waterproof shooting jacket 1937

twentieth century. In turn, the mackintosh has been superseded by the Barbour waxed cotton waterproof jacket and the Gore-Tex lined tweed shooting coat, favoured by many older Guns, and designer outdoor clothing produced by Realtree, Musto and others, which is popular with the younger generation. That said, anything goes on the modern shooting field and wet weather gear might easily include ex-army waterproofs or vintage waterproof clothing handed down from a grandfather or uncle.

Shooting stick

Used by generations of sportsmen for rest purposes when out on the shooting field, the shooting stick – a walking stick which doubles as a portable seat – dates back to the late Victorian period. Early models consisted of a wooden stick with a folding cane seat with handles attached to the extremities. These were superseded by adjustable aluminium sticks with a pointed bottom end for inserting into the ground and a folding leather seat with handles on the top, modelled along the lines of the 'Mills (patent) Aluminium Telescopic Sportsman's Stool', a shooting stick invented by William Mills (who also invented the 'Mills Bomb' hand grenade) during the early Edwardian era. The traditional adjustable aluminium shooting stick with a leather seat continues to be popular today, although some sportsmen now prefer to use extra-lightweight tripod-type sticks with either a solid plastic seat attached or a collapsible fabric seat.

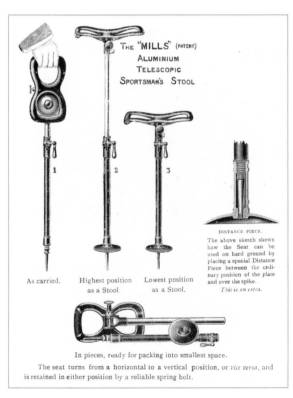

Advertisement for the 'Mills (patent) Aluminium Telescopic Sportsman's Stool' 1903

Essential accessories

Shooting day accessories are many and varied. However, essential items needed when out on the field include a good quality leather cartridge bag or a cartridge belt for carrying cartridges, a cartridge extractor for removing or adjusting any sticking cartridges, a gun slip, a 'priest' (a small truncheon made of wood or antler bone) for despatching any injured game birds, and a game bag or a wooden game carrier for transporting dead game, if rough shooting. If allocating the day's peg placings to the guests, a cartridge place finder can come in useful, too.

Game carrier for transporting dead game birds: courtesy of the GWCT

Shoot Transport

Shoot transport, be it in the form of a horse or a pony or a specially designed carriage or motor car, has been an essential shooting day requirement since the early seventeenth century when men shot while on horseback. Indeed, horses and ponies played an integral part in shoot operations on some northern grouse moors and Scottish estates until the 1960s when all-terrain vehicles took over for carrying sportsmen to remote locations and for recovering game.

Interestingly, in recent years, a number of Scottish sporting properties have reintroduced ponies for shooting and stalking purposes, often as a visitor attraction for overseas guests, particularly those from the United States.

Horses and ponies

Prints of shooting scenes dating back to the seventeenth, eighteenth and early nineteenth centuries usually depict two or three sportsmen mounted on horseback, accompanied by a gamekeeper with his pointers or setters. Although walked-up shooting was the order of the day at this time, horses and ponies were considered necessary for shoot purposes, both as transport to outlying beats and for conveying dead partridges, hares and other game back to the kitchens at a country house.

The introduction of the Continental practice of *battue* during the first half of the nineteenth century, which enabled large numbers of pheasants and partridges to be killed in a day, resulted in an increase in the demand for horses and ponies for shoot operations. It became common practice for a landowner to supply his game department with a horse and cart for carrying foodstuffs, pheasant coops or other items around his estate or for taking dead game to a local railway station for despatch to a game dealer in a distant town. Many employers also began to provide their head gamekeeper with a pony and trap for transport, sometimes with a personal groom, and often supplied horses for their senior keepers or paid them a 'horse allowance' on top of their wages so that they could purchase and maintain a horse or pony of their choice.

Horse drawn station wagons and brakes

From the 1860s onwards, the more progressive landowners started to purchase lightweight station wagons and brakes to collect shooting guests from the nearest railway station and to covey them from a country house to the shooting field. Some enterprising coach builders marketed their own specialist vehicles for this purpose, too. Charles Thorn, for instance, proprietor of the Norfolk Carriage Works at Norwich, produced the 'Thorn's Sporting Char-A-Banc', an open vehicle with bus-like seats which could not only accommodate a party of seven or eight Guns but was capable of travelling over farm tracks and fields at a reasonable speed.

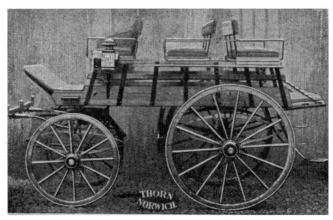

Thorn's Sporting Char-A-Banc

Many landowners also commissioned coach builders and wheelwrights to construct special horse drawn game carts equipped with racks for hanging pheasants and partridges, to convey game killed on low ground shoots from the shooting field to the estate game larder. Usually pulled by a pair of shire horses, these vehicles frequently contained secure storage space for cartridges and many had built-in pull-out tables which could be used by the keepers and beaters at lunchtime.

On moorland shoots, however, horses continued to be used by sportsmen and gamekeepers for travelling back and forth to the grouse moors, while ponies equipped with wickerwork panniers transported dead grouse off the moors at the end of the day. Ponies also played an important part in deer stalking operations. Small Highland ponies, known as 'garrons' were employed in all of the major Scottish deer forests to remove deer carcases from 'the hill' back to the nearest shooting lodge, the carcases being strapped to a specially made saddle.

Horses were regularly used throughout the late nineteenth and the early twentieth centuries by overweight sportsmen for travelling between drives or grouse butts and, exceptionally, provided a seat for the rider at a stand. They were also employed by some head gamekeepers who preferred to be mounted rather than standing when controlling a shoot or giving orders to a group of gamekeepers and beaters.

Sportsmen arriving on horseback on Ramsgill Moor, Yorkshire, August 1934. The gamekeepers, beaters and loaders travelled to the moor on foot accompanied by a horse drawn spring cart which carried guns, ammunition and other necessities

Motorised shoot vehicles

The first motorised shoot vehicles, sometimes referred to as 'shooting brakes' or 'Gun buses', began to appear on the scene at the tail end of the Victorian period. Shortly after the government legalised the use of the motor car on British roads in November 1896, removing the need for a red flag man to walk in front of a car, the well-known motoring pioneer, the Honourable John Scott-Montagu, MP (later 2nd Lord Montagu of Beaulieu), broke new ground by starting to use a car for shooting purposes on the Beaulieu estate in Hampshire. When criticised by other sportsmen for choosing a car instead of horse drawn transport to convey parties of Guns to the shooting field, he commented: 'Eminently useful as it is for many other purposes, the motor car is especially useful for shooting expeditions.'

Lord Iveagh, the Earl of Carnarvon, Mr Henry Chaplin and a number of other well-known shots followed in Mr Montagu's footsteps, purchasing cars for shooting use. However, it was not until King Edward VII acquired a Daimler after ascending the throne in 1901 that motor vehicles became really popular on the shooting field.

Designed for use on unsurfaced roads, either stone, gravel or hardened mud, these early motor cars were large, heavy and of robust construction and could often carry up to ten people. Despite these vehicles costing anything between £600 and £2,500 (between £40,000 and £150,000 at today's prices), sporting landowners would often own two of them, one for transporting a group of Guns, the other for loaders, keepers, dogs and various shooting accoutrements. On many estates, a team of cart horses would be kept on standby on the shooting field in case a car broke down and had to be towed home or pulled out of a piece of soft ground.

Advertisement for the 'Wolseley' Station Car 1904

Keen to capitalise on the growing demand for motorised shoot transport, a number of Edwardian motor manufacturers produced specialist vehicles for use on rough or hilly terrain. Wolseley Siddeley, for example, launched the 'Wolseley' Station Car in 1904, designed for conveying sportsmen and their luggage to shooting lodges and to be driven on hill, field or moor. Rolls-Royce, not to be outdone, followed suit, with the 'Silver Ghost Shooting Brake', built to the purchaser's own specifications by a firm of London coachbuilders. The Commer Motor Co. also manufactured a 'shooting brake', but of bus-like proportions, capable of carrying Guns and their loaders to site in an enclosed carriage, which could double as a luncheon room.

These bespoke shooting vehicles continued to gain popularity throughout the Edwardian era. Indeed, in 1912 King George V, a leading shot of the day, commissioned a 'shooting car' for use on the Sandringham estate in Norfolk. The *Daily Mirror* reported:

'THE KING'S SHOOTING CAR

A novel motor-car for shooting purposes has just been delivered to the King. The car is specially adapted to carry eleven "Guns" and extending over the whole length of it is a canopy fitted with curtains as a protection in stormy weather.'

Shooting cars on the battlefield

Following the outbreak of World War One in 1914, a large number of motorised shoot vehicles were requisitioned by the army for use on the battlefields of France, either as staff cars or as temporary ambulances, or were converted into primitive armoured cars. In some instances, vehicles continued to be driven by their owner or his chauffeur, who usually doubled as his 'batman'. Sadly, many of these beautifully crafted 'shooting cars' did not survive the conflict, being wrecked in battle or abandoned because of mechanical failure.

In the immediate post-war era, few landowners could afford to replace customised shoot vehicles or rebuild shoots to Edwardian standards because of the high taxation imposed by the Lloyd George Government. The more resourceful amongst them acquired ex-army lorries, ambulances or Ford 'Model T' vans, all built for use over rough terrain. Some even purchased bicycles

Ex-army lorry in use as a 'Gun bus' on a Scottish estate c. 1920

equipped with a special gun rack and panniers to enable their guests to ride from a country house to the shooting field, the gamekeepers and loaders also using this mode of transport.

Purpose-built shoot vehicles started to reappear from the mid-1920s onwards, either manufactured to the purchaser's own specification on a Rolls-Royce or a Bentley chassis or available 'off the peg' from Ford and other mass-market car producers. Often complete with rod racks on the outside and gun racks on the inside, and a portable slide-out table for elevenses and luncheon, these 'shooting brakes', as they came to be known, were capable of taking a party of Guns to a remote beat or grouse moor in comfort and at speed, while their ex-army predecessors were kept by many estates in order to convey loaders, beaters, keepers and dog handlers to site.

Due to excessive fuel consumption, many bespoke shoot vehicles were mothballed when World War Two was declared in 1939 and, sometimes, were sent for use for sea defence purposes by patriotic owners or, even, scrapped for the war effort. The First World War vans and lorries fared somewhat better, being pressed into service for military use on the home front.

Ex-army jeeps

Following the cessation of hostilities in 1945, landowners started to purchase ex-army jeeps to convey themselves and their guests to the shooting field. Functional, robust and equipped with four-wheel drive, these vehicles were not only capable of reaching the distant beats of an estate in all weathers but were able to negotiate all but the most inaccessible parts of a grouse moor or deer forest, making pannier ponies and stalking garrons obsolete on a large number of sporting properties.

The jeep, in turn, was superseded by the Land Rover, launched by the Rover Motor Co. in 1948 as an all-terrain four-wheel drive vehicle suitable for shooting, farming and estate purposes. Originally manufactured on a short wheel base with a canvas top, long and short wheel base station wagon versions, with an integral metal roof, were subsequently produced for field sports use to convey parties of Guns or as a gamekeeper's transport. The Land Rover has become something of an iconic vehicle in shooting circles.

Numerous other Land Rover and jeep-type vehicles with a shooting

Land Rovers on the shooting field in snowy conditions c. 1970: courtesy of the GWCT

application have been manufactured since the late 1940s, both by British and overseas car makers. Hugely popular at the present time amongst country folk and town dwellers alike, these range from basic Japanese four-wheel drive jeeps to the luxurious 'Chelsea tractors' made by Range Rover, BMW and other upmarket manufacturers.

In addition to producing four-wheel drive vehicles suitable for field sport use during the late 1940s and the 1950s, the British motor manufacturing industry launched a range of small 'shooting brakes' aimed at the mass market, including the Morris Oxford, the Morris Minor Traveller (manufactured from 1953 until 1971) and the Austin A30 countryman. These 'shooting brakes', although purchased by many estates, were not particularly suitable in off-road situations other than on stone surfaced tracks, and were often just used as runabouts. Equally unsuitable for the shooting field were the larger so-called 'shooting brakes' made during the 1960s by Aston Martin and a number of other prestige car manufacturers.

Historic 'Gun buses'

Notwithstanding the wide range of four-wheel drive vehicles, pick-ups and ATVs that are currently available for shooting purposes, in recent years many shoot owners, particularly those who operate on a commercial basis, have chosen to use old or interesting motors as 'Gun buses' to convey parties of Guns from the main house or lodge to the field. Vintage Land Rovers and ex-army lorries are particular favourites on many shoots, although restored historic 'shooting brakes' often rescued from old farm buildings or country house outhouses, veteran cars, early lorries and even old motor coaches, really do add a certain style and glamour to the proceedings on a shoot day. It goes without saying that were it not for members of the shooting fraternity putting these vehicles to good use on the field, many would still be rotting away in the countryside or languishing in the sterile atmosphere of a museum.

Refurbished ex-army truck with a purpose-built 'Gun compartment' in use as a 'Gun bus' on a Dorset shoot

Customs

Various shooting day customs have developed over the years, ranging from giving a gamekeeper a gratuity at the end of a shoot day, either in cash or in kind (such as surplus cartridges or a brace of rabbits or pheasants, etc.), to 'blooding' a novice shot by anointing his or her forehead with blood from their first kill. Other than tipping and shoot photography, the great majority of these time honoured rituals have now gone by the wayside.

One of the earliest shooting day customs, which apparently was common at the beginning of the nineteenth century, was the practice of the head gamekeeper on an estate to enter the dining room of a country house at the end of dinner and to announce the day's bag to the Guns. George Tickner, an American, who was staying with the 5th Duke of Bedford at Woburn Abbey during this period observed an event of this kind and recorded that he had witnessed: 'A curious aristocratic ritual which took place at the end of dinner when the cloth had been removed, and the gamekeeper appeared in all his paraphernalia and rendered his account: four hundred and four partridges and pheasants had fallen to eleven Guns.'

Tipping

The most important shooting day custom of all, the practice of tipping a gamekeeper, appears to date back to the early days of driven game shooting when the head gamekeeper on an estate (rather than the host) was responsible for placing the Guns and wealthy guests were not only prepared to pay him substantial sums of money in advance in order to secure the best positions, but also to give him a generous gratuity at the end of a two- or three-day shoot. Despite a number of fair minded landowners trying to stamp out 'bribes' of this nature by paying their gamekeeping staff an annual bonus in lieu of tips or by installing a tip box in the gun room or elsewhere and instructing guests to put money in it (for distribution amongst the gamekeepers at the end of the season) instead of handing it over to favoured individuals, tipping became an accepted ritual and has survived until the present time.

Back in the Edwardian era, when a head gamekeeper earned in the region of £2 a week, it was not unusual for him to be given a tip of £5 or £10 by a wealthy guest. A beat or under-keeper at this time, who might be paid around £1 a week, could expect a tip of at least £1, while a trainee keeper, earning perhaps 10/- a week, would often be tipped between 5/- (25p) and 7/6 (37½p). However, blanket-type tips of this nature have gradually been replaced by bag-related tips over the course of the twentieth century, with a modern-day gamekeeper usually receiving an initial 'gift' of £20 plus an additional tip of £10 for every hundred birds shot. It goes without saying, of course, that tips are regarded as an important part of a gamekeeper's income.

The shoot photograph

Something of a tradition on many of the great shoots, the custom of taking a photograph of a party of Guns, either before setting out for a day on the field or at the end of the day beside the bag, dates back to the late 1850s when our Victorian forbears developed a love affair with the camera, then something of a novelty. By the late nineteenth century, shoot photographs had become well established, with smartly dressed Guns and their ladies, wearing suitable outdoor attire, being 'snapped' for posterity at lunchtime or during the afternoon. Photographers from *Country Life* and other upmarket photo journals began to visit well-known shoots at this time, taking both portrait and action shots for the benefit of their readers, particularly those resident overseas. Later, members of the shooting fraternity purchased their own cameras, taking DIY pictures on the field for the family album, a practice which had become commonplace by the 1920s and has continued until the present time. That said, over the past thirty years or so with the growth in commercial shooting, there has been a resurgence in high quality professional shoot

Shoot photograph taken at Broadlands, Hampshire on 1 December 1936. Guns include German Ambassador, Herr Von Ribbentrop (second from left wearing bow tie), Colonel George Philippi (far left) and the owner of Broadlands, Lord Mount Temple (third from left). The bag taken on the day amounted to 342 pheasants, 3 partridges, 10 hares, 5 rabbits and 7 pigeons

photography, with specialist photographers taking pictures either for private use or for publication in the sporting press.

The 'sweep'

Increasingly popular in recent years, the sweepstake or 'sweep' which takes place during lunch on some shoots to guess the size of the day's bag or the total number of shots fired, is a relatively modern shooting day custom which appears to date back to the mid-twentieth century. 'Sweeps' are generally confined to the Guns present on the day, although it is not unknown for everyone involved in a shoot day to participate – Guns, wives, keepers, loaders, beaters and pickers-up – providing substantial prize money for the winner. Etiquette-wise, it is considered to be bad form to hold a 'sweep' if any Gun present is known to be opposed to gambling. Interestingly, in the early 1930s, the 2nd Duke of Westminster often invited a bookmaker to attend his shoots in order that he could stand behind certain Guns on a drive, in turn, and enable them to bet on the odds on a bird coming over!

The Game Book

Considered to be almost as important as the family Bible on some sporting estates during the Edwardian era, the game book is kept to provide an accurate record of each shooting day and normally records the size and variety of the bag, the names of the Guns present, the beats shot over and the weather. Some game books also include pick-up details, gamekeepers' names, the number of beaters hired on the day, game disposal lists and other items of information. In times past, it was usual to keep the game book on display in the gun room, the billiard room or the library of a great house for the benefit of shooting guests, but in recent years it has become the practice to keep such books in an estate office, often under secure conditions. Today, many estates

Cover of a traditional leather bound game book

and commercial shoots keep a computerised game book, both for accounting purposes and to enable bag data to be supplied to potential clients.

The first game books began to appear during the mid-eighteenth century and usually recorded little more than an annual or a daily bag figure. For example, the game book for the Flixton estate in Suffolk, which commences in 1775, simply states that between 1 September 1775 and 6 January 1776, a total of 115 partridges, 18 pheasants and 38 hares were shot over a period of forty-six days. Neither the Guns nor the shoot locations are listed.

Early printed game books with tabulated columns for daily bag figures and quarry species came on the market during the first two decades of the nineteenth century, either with plain or leather covers. These were gradually superseded during the Victorian period by large leather bound gilt-edged tomes designed with a page layout to record a multitude of shoot day details. Game books have been simplified and reduced in size since this time and can now be purchased either in hardback or loose leaf format.

Dedicated game books are not only kept by sportsmen but also by gamekeepers, land agents and others associated with shoot management. For shoot day recording purposes, they fall into the following categories:

The estate game book

Maintained either by the owner of an estate, his land agent or his head gamekeeper, the estate game book usually records details of daily bags and baskets taken on a property, lists beats or locations where shooting took place, lakes, lochs, beats or pools where fish were landed, who was out shooting and fishing on the day, and, occasionally, prevailing weather conditions. Although regarded as fairly accurate documents by sportsmen, estate game books can occasionally list lower bag figures than those actually taken, particularly if kept by a sporting lessee whose annual rental is based to an extent on bags and baskets taken in previous years.

The personal game book

Kept by an individual sportsman, this is the most accurate and detailed game book of all, containing numbers of game shot and fish caught, weights of salmon, sea trout and other fish taken and the flies used, the state of rivers, lakes or lochs,

GAME RECORD.

DATE	BY WHOM SHOT	WHERE	PTARMIGAN	HARES	RABBITS	PARTRIDGES	PHEASANTS (Cocks)	PHEASANTS (Hens)	WOODCOCK	GROUSE	WILD FOWL	SNIPE	DAILY TOTAL
Oct 2nd	Mr Frank Mayor Vaughan Colonel Burns Beg Crabbe J.B.H. Self J. Peel B. Peel Teldy C.S.H Self	The Cob Pullton + Bowland		2						86	4 golden plover		42
Oct 16		Plover Hall		10	8	20							58
Dec 20th	Mr French Colonel Dixon E. Platt G. Banks J.B.H. Hugo Self	Penrhyn Castle Bangor		40	1	160					1		202
" 21st	Mr French Colonel Dixon E Platt G. Banks J.B.H E Yoxlle Broadhurst Hugo Self	— " —		9		291							300
" 23rd	Mr French E. Yoxlle Broadhurst E Platt G. Banks J.B.H Hugo Tom Self	— " —		12		200		1			37	1	251
" 26th	C. Cheetenham Edmund to Philip Wilbraham C.P.H Self	Somerford Boolties		4	6	1	14						25

Total for week ending_____19

Pages from a personal game book dated 1912 kept by Benjamin Sumner Hoare of Holmes Chapel, Cheshire. The game record faces…

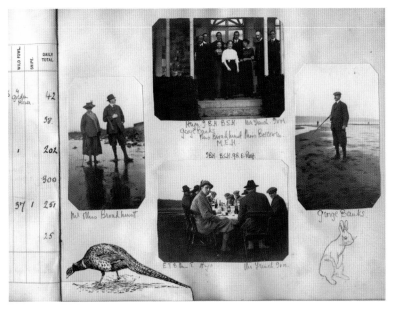

…the photographs which were taken at the shooting party at Penrhyn Castle in December 1912. Both photographs courtesy of Chris North

weights of stags and hinds killed and information about stags antlers, weather conditions, and noting the names of other sportsmen out on the shooting field or the water and gamekeepers or ghillies in attendance. These books sometimes also include observations on wildlife sighted, particularly eagles and other birds of prey, names and breeds of dogs out on a shoot, photographs or sketches of shooting parties or landscapes, and small anecdotes about deer stalks or other sporting activities.

Game cards

Although not a game book as such, game cards were introduced in the mid-nineteenth century to provide a record of the day's sport for each Gun in a shooting party, either for transcription into a personal game book at a later date or simply to be kept as a souvenir. Early game cards were fairly basic, often little more than a piece of plain card or paper bearing bag details written out in copperplate, but over the years cards have evolved into small printed booklets, usually with an illustrated cover showing a local view, game birds or a map of a shoot. Game cards can include a wide variety of information but typically list the day's bag, beats shot over, Guns out on the shooting field and weather conditions.

Game Meat Disposal and Processing

Game meat, the end product of the shooting day, was traditionally restricted to the tables of the aristocracy and the landed gentry, or members of the upper middle classes who were rich enough to purchase pheasants or partridges from a licensed game dealer or via the black market. However, following the introduction of the breech-loading shot gun in the mid-nineteenth century, which enabled a sportsman to kill a large amount of birds within a relatively short space of time, game became a much more readily available commodity and found an immediate market amongst the newly emergent Victorian urban middle classes.

The game cart

Game at this time was picked-up from the field and hung in braces on racks on an open horse drawn game cart at the end of a shoot, then conveyed back to an

Pheasants hung on a game rack in 'feather' in the traditional manner

The game cart on an Essex shoot c. 1955

estate game larder where some would be set aside for house use and the remainder either given away locally or despatched to a game dealer. The latter game would frequently be sent quite a distance from the nearest railway station to a game dealer in a large town in the guards van of a train, either tied in braces or packed in hampers. This practice was not at all conducive to hygiene as guards vans were usually heated by a stove, and might also contain dogs belonging to passengers, farm produce and parcels as well as game.

Having reached the game dealer's premises, game would either be put in a larder for storage, despatched to regular customers or hung outside the dealer's shop, exposed to the elements, small birds and insects, while awaiting purchase by passing shoppers. Traditionally game was sold in 'fur and feather' and plucked or skinned and gutted by the purchaser rather than being prepared in an 'oven ready' state by the dealer.

This system of game transportation and processing remained much the same until the late twentieth century, although by this time game transport had changed from horse and train to tractor and trailer, van and lorry and dealers were using walk-in cold rooms for storage rather than tiled larders and were starting to sell game birds, in particular, in oven-ready form, or even in breast or leg portions, and were retailing potted game meat, pâté and game cat food. Further, a general improvement in public hygiene standards in all areas meant that game for human consumption was now handled more carefully and was less exposed to germs, insects and rodents.

Hanging up game in the game larder at the end of the day c. 1960s: courtesy of the GWCT

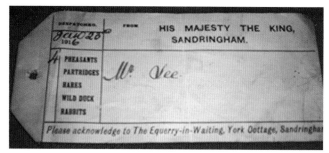

Tag made of waxed linen which was affixed to game given away by
King George V when shooting at Sandringham

Game and poultry on display for Christmas outside a game dealer's premises at
High Wycombe, Buckinghamshire 1938

Game meat hygiene regulations

However, following the passage of the Food Safety Act in 1990 and the subsequent implementation of The Wild Game Meat (Hygiene and Inspection) Regulations in 1995, it became necessary for game dealers and other businesses selling, processing, transporting and exporting game to obtain a licence for their premises as well as to comply with recommendations made by local authority food hygiene inspectors and to adhere to voluntary guidelines set down in The National Game Dealers Association Code of Good Game Handling. Additional legislation brought in over the past decade or so to comply with EU rules has been extended to cover the game handling and processing activities of shoot operators, gamekeepers and others on private estate premises, both on the field and in the game larder.

Indeed, it has now become obligatory for game to be removed from the shooting field as quickly as possible, cooled and hung in a game larder in a controlled temperature of 4° C or lower for small game carcases and 7° C or lower for large game carcases such as deer or wild boar. Further, it is recommended that estates handling large quantities of game should install a chiller or refrigeration unit in their game handling area.

Oven-ready duck, partridges and pheasants hygienically packaged and displayed in a chiller cabinet at the premises of J&J Longley Wiltshire Game, Tisbury

Food safety and traceability

In 2006, in the interests of food safety and traceability, the EU decreed that anyone producing and supplying wild game to a commercial dealer or related business should be trained in anatomy, physiology, pathology, food and animal hygiene legislation and other relevant areas to a standard acceptable to the Food Standards Agency and issued with a Trained Hunter Identification Number, the only exceptions being persons producing small quantities of game for personal consumption, as gifts, to a local consumer or to a local retailer directly supplying the final consumer.

Despite being considered somewhat intrusive by some of the more traditional sportsmen, this legislation has enabled shoots not only to sell game to supermarket chains, who demand rigorous traceability procedures for all meat products, but also to export game meat to Europe and elsewhere in the world. Indeed, in recent years game meat has become increasingly popular with the general public, with supermarkets, market stalls and other retail outlets stocking pheasants, partridges, pigeons, duck, venison and wild boar or selling game pies, sausages, faggots, pâtés or other processed dishes. Game can be found on the menu in many restaurants and public houses at the present time too.

Shoot Operating Costs

Running a shoot has always been a costly business, particularly in times past when members of the aristocracy and the landed gentry competed with each other to see who could provide the biggest pheasant bag in one day or the most lavish hospitality on the field. Indeed, prior to the 1970s virtually every shoot was operated a loss, with expenditure far exceeding income.

Early nineteenth century estate records frequently include references to shoot costs, albeit in the form of an overall figure rather than as an itemised account. The Steward's Account for the Sturminster estate in Dorset, for example, reveals that in 1801 a total of £21/16/4 (£21.82) was spent on game preservation and shooting, which included the gamekeeper's salary of £10 per annum. The General Account for the 10,000 acre Audley End estate in Essex for 1825, however, not only records that out of a total annual expenditure of

£4,307/16/7½ (£4,307.83) the owner, the 2nd Lord Brayebrooke, lavished £732/14/9½ (£732.74) on the shoot. In comparison he spent £472/8/2 (£472.41) on housekeeping and wages in the mansion house and £174/9/6 (£174.47½) on running the stables.

SHOOT COSTS AT LIVERMERE PARK IN 1858

Surviving accounts for the Livermere Park estate in Suffolk for the period 1 February 1858 to 1 February 1859 record that the total operating cost of the shoot was £183/16/9 (£183.84). This figure can be broken down into the following payments and purchases:

Keeper's wages for 12 months	£91/4/0 (£91.20)
Paid as per keeper's book, bills for powder and shot, corn for dogs, game largesse etc. etc.	£55/9/6 (£55.47½)
Certificate for keepers	£1/8/6 (£1.42½)
Tar for keepers	£1/1/0 (£1.05)
House rent for keepers	£4
Firing for keepers	£1/10/0 (£1.50)
Clothes for keepers	£3/15/0 (£3.75)
Sundries	£25/8/9 (£25.44)

Remarkably, the Livermere Park shoot appears to have been self-financing. The income for 1858–9 equalled the expenditure incurred on the shoot outgoings. This sum was derived solely from the sale of the following items of game:

384 pheasants @ 2/6 (12½p)	£48
1,451 partridges @ 9d (4p)	£54/8/3 (£54.41½)
219 hares @ 2/- (10p)	£21/18/0 (£21.90)
304 rabbits @ 6d (2½p)	£7/12/0 (£7.60)
10 woodcock @ 1/6 (7½p)	15/- (£0.75p)
12 wildfowl @ 1/6 (7½p)	18/- (£0.90p)
2,011 rabbits killed by warreners	£50/5/6 (£50.27½)

Shoot outgoings inevitably increased from the mid-Victorian period onwards as more and more landowners changed over from walked-up to driven shooting. It now became necessary to employ a large gamekeeping staff to rear vast quantities of pheasants and partridges annually, while farm rentals were reduced in order for land to be cultivated in the best interests of game preservation rather than for optimum commercial gain. Further costs were incurred through the provision of residential hospitality for shooting guests, many of whom came with a retinue of servants in tow to look after their personal needs, who also needed food and accommodation.

Edwardian-style shoot expenditure

By the Early Edwardian era, running a shoot on a 'money no object' basis had become an extremely expensive business, involving substantial annual financial

Shoot Account for the Broadlands estate, Hampshire dated 23 July 1927. Outgoings listed include keepers' wages, employees' National Insurance Stamps and payments made to partridge nest finders

losses. For example, in 1901 the 4th Duke of Sutherland, then the largest landowner in Western Europe, paid out a total of £1,334/9/9 (£1,334.49) on his shoot on the 17,000 acre Lilleshall Hall estate in Shropshire, but only received £148/8/8 (£148.43) in return from the sale of rabbits and hares and the re-sale of broody hens to farmers. He rarely shot over the property more than ten times a year due to sporting commitments on his other English and Scottish estates. However his guests, usually members of the royal family or high ranking noblemen, could expect to bring down between 800 and 1,000 pheasants in a day along with partridges, hares, rabbits and a small number of woodcock.

From the time of his accession in 1892 until his death in 1913, the 4th Duke of Sutherland maintained incredibly detailed accounts for the Lilleshall shoot. Miscellaneous items purchased in 1901 include four Clumber spaniels for £31/10/0 (£31.50), one night dog for £6/6/0 (£6.30), a new gun for £15 and numerous quantities of turnips for distribution in the woods during snowy weather for the rabbits to feed upon. In 1903, he paid his head keeper £122/8/0 (£122.40), comprising a salary of £90 per annum, £30 for the keep of a horse and an allowance of £2/8/0 (£2.40) for soap and candles. In the same year he spent a total of £538/1/9 (£538.09) on game food, £70/17/6 (£70.87½) for broody hens for rearing purposes, £50 for a new game wagon and £87/5/0 (£87.25) for the keep of seven retrievers, three night dogs and four spaniels. His fourteen gamekeepers at this time were not allowed to accept tips but were given a gratuity of £3 per annum from the shoot budget instead.

Shoot outgoings in the 1960s and '70s

By contrast, nearly six decades later in 1959, Earl Mountbatten of Burma, owner of the 6,000 acre Broadlands estate at Romsey in Hampshire, spent a total of £6,351 on running the Broadlands shoot, the highest outgoings being the gamekeepers' salaries which amounted to £2,228 and the beaters' wages at £555. He organised twenty shoot days during the course of the season, which yielded a total bag of 3,202 pheasants, 61 partridges, 332 hares, 10 rabbits, 139 wild duck, 16 woodcock and 1 snipe. Guns included HRH Prince Philip, Duke of Edinburgh; the Prime Minister, Harold Macmillan; the Defence Minister, Duncan Sandys; and the American Ambassador, John Hay Witney.

Earl Mountbatten, who was keen to turn Broadlands into one of Britain's top shoots, gradually built up the shoot over the next two decades prior to his assassination by the IRA in 1979. He increased the number of days and formed a syndicate of paying Guns in order to defray some of the costs. His annual shoot expenditure increased correspondingly, rising to £11,385 in 1967 and £23,084 by 1974. Nevertheless, in 1974, the shoot made an overall loss of just under £4,000. Indeed, by 1977, Earl Mountbatten was so concerned about the state of the shoot finances that he wrote to his head gamekeeper, Harry Grass, telling him that 'the farm must make the greatest possible profit to help the shoot'.

Shoot operating costs have, inevitably, increased dramatically over the past forty years or so, despite the fact that during this period many shoots have disbanded labour intensive on-site game bird rearing systems in favour of purchasing pheasants and partridges from game farms for release at poult stage, and have taken advantage of the latest veterinary medication products to avoid adult bird losses. Many shoots have provided gamekeepers with quad bikes and other mechanical labour-saving equipment in order for them to be able to carry out their duties more efficiently. Today, where a shoot is run along commercial lines with days let to parties of paying Guns, it is not unusual for the annual turnover to exceed £5,000,000.

SHOOTING IN
ENGLAND AND WALES

SHOOTING HAS BEEN A POPULAR SPORT in England and Wales for over three and a half centuries. Sportsmen have not only gone out in pursuit of the pheasant, the partridge and the red grouse (long regarded as the three principal game birds) during this period but also the woodcock, the snipe, the black grouse, the hare, the rabbit, various species of wildfowl and other more peripheral quarry. The great bustard (now extinct), the quail, the landrail (corn-crake) and the wheatear were all shot as game birds in bygone days, too. Game birds have received legal protection of one kind and another since medieval times and have been reared and released for shooting purposes for around 250 years.

Grouse shooting party walking to the butts on Stean Moor, North Yorkshire c. 1950

Partridge

Considered to be the principal British game bird until the mid-Victorian period, the English or grey partridge has been hawked, netted and shot by sportsmen since the Middle Ages. The grey partridge has been preserved for sport for centuries, both through vermin control and poaching prevention and by the implementation of successive Acts of Parliament passed to protect game birds. Partridges can be legally shot between 1 September and 1 February, a season established under the terms of the Game Act of 1831.

Sportsmen experimented with artificial grey partridge rearing using broody hens for incubation purposes as a means of increasing stocks as early as the late eighteenth century. Hand rearing did not become general practice until the late Victorian period when a number of top shoot owners implemented hand rearing in order to obtain large bags of driven partridges. Hand-reared partridges, however, were considered to be less sporting than wild birds, so this mode of preservation was eschewed by many of the leading shots of the day.

Shoot owners instead used nest management in order to preserve the grey partridge for sport, a practice that was pioneered in the mid-eighteenth century (both for pheasants and for partridges) and which continued to be operated on some estates until the 1950s. Under this system a 'nest payment' of 1/- (5p) per nest was made to farm labourers and others for reporting the locations of nests in fields and hedgerows to a gamekeeper, so that he could keep a watching brief over the nests in spring and early summer, monitoring hatching and the keeping an eye on the young partridges. On many large sporting properties, the 'nest payments' were given out at an annual supper, held to thank farm staff for cooperating with the gamekeeping team.

Nest management continued to be the favoured method of grey partridge preservation until the late Victorian period when Mr Pearson Gregory, sporting tenant on the Duke of Grafton's Euston estate in Suffolk, developed the 'Euston System' for increasing and improving the partridge stocks on a shoot. Under this system, partridge eggs were removed from nests and replaced with artificial eggs, then incubated beneath broody hens until the point of chipping, when they were returned to nests for hatching.

Advantages gained by using the 'Euston System' to rear grey partridges included the minimisation of nest losses through bad weather and vermin destruction and the ability to improve stocks by moving eggs from one nest to another. Indeed, many gamekeepers operating this method of preservation exchanged eggs with neighbouring estates in order to obtain new blood, or even travelled by express train to London and swapped a consignment of eggs with a keeper from a distant county such as Yorkshire, Hampshire or Devon at a mainline railway station. The 'Euston System' continued to be used extensively throughout England until the late 1930s.

Grey partridge stocks began to decline in many districts following the end of World War One in 1918. The recession of the 1920s and '30s caused a large number of estates to be put down to grass and the birds disappeared where they had once been common. However, they still survived in large numbers where arable farming predominated.

The grey partridge suffered again in the wake of World War Two. The introduction of new arable farming methods, designed to optimise food

Pair of English or grey partridges in the snow: courtesy of David Mason

production, did much to destroy the habitat of the bird. Large scale hedgerow and bank removal, stubble burning, silage cutting in May, artificial fertilisers and chemical weed killer sprays which destroy the insects on which the birds live, all took their toll on grey partridge survival rates.

Sadly, the grey partridge became increasingly scarce throughout the country until the late 1990s when a number of landowners implemented 'grey partridge recovery projects' in an attempt to build up stocks of grey partridges on their properties. Sympathetic farming practices, habitat enhancement, bag limits, the occasional temporary shooting ban, combined with the release of artificially reared grey partridges from game farms, have all led to a return of the birds in significant numbers on the sporting estates involved, with the result that good daily bags can now be obtained on walked-up and driven shoots.

The Hungarian grey partridge

Grey partridges were first imported into Britain from Hungary and other parts of Central Europe during the mid-nineteenth century in order to bolster up the native stocks which were being decimated by overshooting in some areas. The birds and their eggs could be obtained over the counter from dealers in Leadenhall Market in London from the 1850s onwards, or purchased on a private basis from advertisers in journals such as *The Field*.

Advertisement for Hungarian grey partridges 1907

In the late Victorian and Edwardian periods, major landowners were turning down large numbers of Hungarian grey partridges every year with the sole purpose of obtaining increased bags. For example, the 6th Duke of Portland more than doubled his annual bag at Welbeck Abbey in Nottinghamshire in the late 1890s through the introduction of as many as 1,200 birds at a time. Sir William Gordon Cumming was similarly successful doubling his bag at Altyre in Scotland using this method in only three seasons.

Other landowners at this time, including Alexander Pitt-Rivers at Rushmore in Wiltshire, the Earl of Ellesmere at Stetchworth in Cambridgeshire and Sir John Gladstone at Fasque in Kincardineshire, achieved equally good increased bags using imported Hungarian grey partridge eggs which were hatched out under fowls.

Hungarian grey partridges and partridge eggs continued to be imported into Britain until 1939. One supplier, 'The Country Gentleman's Association' of Letchworth, charged £13/10/0 (£13.50) per hundred eggs at this time and was prepared to quote a price upon application for birds which had been 'penned on clean sweet meadow land for about ten days to recover from the effects of their journey from Hungary and to become acclimatised'.

The Hungarian grey partridge trade was suspended during World War Two then stopped entirely following the cessation of hostilities in 1945 when Hungary was absorbed into communist Eastern Europe. Today, the English or grey partridge, considered by many to be a native species, is of largely Hungarian ancestry.

The French or 'red-legged' partridge
Commonly found on sporting properties throughout Great Britain today, the French or 'red-legged' partridge was introduced into England during the late eighteenth century as an additional partridge quarry species after overshooting and netting in some parts of East Anglia and the south-eastern counties had reduced stocks of native grey partridges to perilous levels. Rather than putting down live birds, landowners imported partridge eggs from France and hatched them out beneath broody hens in order to boost partridge numbers on their ground. Two adjoining Suffolk landowners, the Marquess of Hertford of Sudbourne and Peter Thelluson of Rendelsham, are credited with the first

introduction of French partridge eggs into England in 1770. They were followed by the Duke of Richmond at Goodwood in Sussex who purchased a consignment of 800 partridge eggs from France at a cost of £14/16/0 (£14.80) in 1774, and his neighbour, Sir Henry Fetherstonhaugh, Bt. at Uppark, who obtained eggs from France in 1776.

Surviving records for the Rendelsham estate indicate that it took several decades for the French partridge stocks to build up to a level that a reasonable bag could be obtained. For example in 1806, 112 'red-legged' partridges were shot on the property in comparison with 1,815 grey partridges. The birds could have been more successful if some neighbouring landowners had not instructed their gamekeepers to shoot them as vermin.

Throughout the early nineteenth century the French partridge was gradually introduced into southern and eastern England, particularly in the corn growing districts, to provide an additional quarry species for sportsmen. The birds were first released in West Suffolk in 1823 when Lord de Ros and Lord Alvanley

French or 'red-legged' partridge: courtesy of David Mason

imported eggs from France, which were hatched and turned down in the Culford area. French partridge had reached the western edge of Hampshire by 1834 when the Earl of Malmesbury put down several pairs on the Heron Court estate near Christchurch.

By 1900, the French partridge could be found throughout much of England and in some parts of Scotland. The birds were now being artificially reared on many estates, with the stocks regularly being supplemented and improved by the importation of fresh birds and eggs from France and other countries. It has been said that on some estates at this time French partridges might

Walked-up partridge shooting. Etching by Howitt 1819

account for between twenty-five and fifty per cent of the daily partridge bag taken on specific beats.

French partridges and eggs continued to be brought into Britain on a regular basis up until the start of World War Two in 1939 in order to 'bolster up' the thriving residual populations that had been established in many areas of the country. Thereafter, the birds readily adapted to the new arable farming methods that were introduced in the wake of the war which, sadly, did much to destroy the natural habitat of the grey partridge. The French or 'red-legged' partridge subsequently took over as the principal partridge quarry species on the majority of British sporting properties and remains so today.

Shooting partridges

Prior to the introduction of driving during the Victorian period, partridges were traditionally walked-up and shot over dogs during early autumn, with sportsmen tramping through the stubbles or root fields from dawn to late afternoon in pursuit of a couple of brace of birds. From the 'First' (of September) onwards, according to Archibald Weyland Ruggles-Brise who began to shoot on the family estate in Essex in 1866: 'Small parties consisting of two or three Guns, used to be up long before breakfast, and, accompanied by one or two steady old pointers and setters, would work the stubbles for a respectable bag; later on sport would be continued in cover, a rule being made that shooting should not be continued after 4 p.m., thus giving the birds a chance to feed.'

Shooting driven partridges in Hampshire, September 1984: courtesy of the GWCT

On some estates, the partridge season was opened by the head gamekeeper on 1 September and was shot over by him and his colleagues until late September or early October, until the owner returned from his Scottish shooting quarters, having spent the summer and part of the autumn grouse shooting, salmon fishing and deer stalking. In these circumstances, it was not uncommon for partridges to be sent by rail from England for consumption in a Scottish shooting lodge. In times past, an estate was occasionally operated solely as a partridge shoot, pheasants being shot on sight as vermin. Properties of this kind were traditionally known as a 'Partridge Manor'.

Partridge driving

Partridge driving – the practice of moving partridges towards a party of Guns using a team of beaters rather than walking-up the birds over dogs – appears to have started in a small way on shoots in Essex, Suffolk and Cambridgeshire during the mid-nineteenth century. Surviving game books from this period record that driving was first carried out in Essex at Runwell Hall on 31 January 1844, when a team of five Guns – each using two muzzle-loaders – accounted for a bag of thirty-six brace of partridges; and had been adopted on the Hylands and Writtle estates in the Chelmsford area by 1861. Driving is reputed to have been implemented by Lord Huntingfield on the Heveningham Hall estate in Suffolk in about 1845, and had obviously reached Cambridgeshire by 1850. An entry in the game register for Cheveley Park (then owned by the 5th Duke of Rutland) dated 11 November 1850 notes: 'Partridges very wild; but by driving them round and backwards and forwards we had some excellent sport.'

According to Captain Aymer Maxwell, in his book *Partridges and Partridge Manors*, driving was first introduced into Suffolk to enable elderly sportsmen, who found walking all day in pursuit of French partridges somewhat tiring, to shoot the birds in a less physically strenuous manner. Initially, the Guns stood behind a hedge with their backs to the beaters and shot at the partridges after they had passed over – not the easiest of tasks or the best way to achieve big bags. It was soon realised, however, that much better results could be obtained if the Guns faced the drive and shot at the partridges as they came towards them, a system that was eventually adopted on partridge shoots in many parts of the country.

Sportsman shooting driven partridges from an improvised butt made of turves c. 1920.
Temporary partridge shooting butts were also constructed using hurdles or bales of straw

That said, driven partridge shooting did not really take off until the late Victorian period when the leading shoot owners of the day had started to actively compete with each other for the biggest daily bags. The 2nd Earl of Leicester, for example, introduced partridge driving on his estate at Holkham in Norfolk in 1875, and rapidly increased the annual partridge bag; Lord Ashburton began driving at The Grange at Alresford in Hampshire in the early 1880s with similar results; Lord Mount Temple held his first partridge drive at Broadlands in Hampshire on 29 October 1892; while the 6th Duke of Portland experimented with driving on the Welbeck Abbey estate in Nottinghamshire in 1894 and 1895 and implemented the practice on a large scale basis in 1896.

By the Edwardian era driving had superseded walking-up as the principal method of partridge shooting on all but the smallest of sporting estates, wherever stocks were sufficiently large enough to make it viable. Driven partridge shooting waned somewhat during the mid-twentieth century because of reduced partridge population levels, but has become increasingly popular again over the past thirty years or so. Some commercial shoots are managed specifically for partridges (French or 'red-legged' rather than English or grey) or have dedicated partridge beats.

Driven partridge shooting amid the chalk pits at Holborough, Kent 1933.
The caption on the back of the photograph reads:'Waiting for the drive'.
In the background are seen workmen working on the chalk face

THE PARTRIDGE

'The partridge, like the pheasant, feeds during the summer-season in the cornfields, and is to be found, during the winter, in the turnips, and in the brakes, and other coverts. The pointer and setter, with or without spaniels, are the dogs appropriate to this game; and a brace, or a leash, of the former, are a very handsome attendance for one or two shooters. According to the rules of Sporting, not always so well observed as is necessary, by hot-headed juvenile Gunners, everyone should wait patiently for his own bird, when they rise singly, rising on his own side. A bird rising between two Gunners may be, in course, shot at by both. When the covey, being flushed, rises together, every Gunner should mark a bird, and watch its fall; but it is held unfair to "flank the covey", or fire into the thickest of them, without aiming at a particular bird. One great object, never to be neglected by shooters in company, is to BEWARE OF ACCIDENTS.'

Henry Alken

The National Sports of Great Britain 1821

Pheasant

Something of a rarity in many districts until the nineteenth century, the pheasant was, nevertheless, introduced into Great Britain prior to the Norman Conquest (possibly by the Romans) and has been highly prized by sportsmen since the medieval period when hawks were used to capture and kill the birds for the table. The pheasant has been actively preserved for shooting purposes since the reign of King Charles II (1660–1685) and has been protected by a succession of game laws since the twelfth century. The shooting season for pheasants runs from 1 October until 1 February.

Sporting landowners carried out pheasant preservation through vermin control and poaching prevention until the mid-eighteenth century when the practice of nest management was introduced as a means of artificially increasing stocks. Similar to the system used for the English or grey partridge, farm workers and others were given a 'nest payment' for informing a gamekeeper of the whereabouts of a pheasant's nest in order that he could keep watch over it during the rearing season and monitor the progress of the hatch until the chicks had reached poult stage. In areas where pheasants were scarce, it was not uncommon for the 'nest payment' to considerably exceed the 1/- (5p) that was paid out for a partridge nest. For example on the Buscot estate in Berkshire in 1796, men were paid 2/6d (12½p) per pheasant nest found at a time when the average weekly wage was only around 8/- (40p).

In addition to implementing nest management systems to increase pheasant stocks, some of the leading landowners of the day started to artificially rear and release pheasants for sport during the mid-eighteenth century, building secure pheasantries and using broody hens to incubate pheasant eggs which had been collected from nests in woods and hedgerows. Expensive to operate and labour intensive, this method of preservation was not widely adopted until the early Victorian period when Prince Albert, the Prince Consort, popularised *battue* or driven pheasant shooting amongst aristocracy and the landed gentry, thus creating a demand for large numbers of pheasants on sporting estates throughout the country. Landowners and game farmers continued to rear pheasants in this manner, using broody hens or bantams for incubation until the 1960s and '70s, despite the fact that primitive paraffin-fired incubators for hatching out pheasant eggs had been on the market since around 1890.

Pheasant rearing, in fact, did not really undergo any kind of modernisation

Male pheasant: courtesy of David Mason

process until the 1960s when some of the more progressive landowners and game farmers, influenced both by the renewed interest in large scale driven pheasant shooting and rising labour costs, began to use incubators and hatchers for hatching out pheasant eggs and electric, gas or paraffin-powered brooder units and runs such as the 'Rupert Brooder' or the 'Fordingbridge System', developed by the Game Conservancy, for housing young chicks for the six weeks before they were moved to a release pen. At the same time, increasing use was made of the intensive pheasant rearing system, operated along the lines of a deep litter poultry system, whereby chicks are kept in sections in a large shed or a disused farming building before being prepared for release.

By the mid-1970s, virtually every estate that continued to rear pheasants in-house had changed over from the broody hen method of artificial rearing to the various modern systems that had become available. Since the late 1980s, however, the great majority of shoot owners have purchased pheasant poults from game farms for release purposes rather than rearing birds on site. In some cases they buy day-old chicks for rearing and eventual release on the shooting field.

The 'setting pen' yard at Yattendon Court, Berkshire 1937. The broody hens used for pheasant egg incubation are tethered alongside the rows of nest boxes. There were 5,000 pheasants reared annually at Yattendon during the 1930s using this method of incubation

Day-old pheasant chicks in an incubator: courtesy of the Game Farmers' Association

Shooting

Pheasants were walked-up and shot over dogs in the time honoured manner until the early years of nineteenth century when driven pheasant shooting was introduced on a number of leading English estates. Initially slow to take off, this method of shooting gradually increased in popularity during the first part of the Victorian period and by 1875 had superseded walked-up pheasant shooting on virtually every sporting property in England and on many in Scotland, Ireland and Wales.

From the mid-1870s until the outbreak of World War One in 1914, driven pheasant shooting dominated all of the great country house shoots, other than on sporting properties that were operated primarily as partridge manors or had dedicated partridge beats. Shooting did not begin until November on many estates, the shots of the day being of the opinion that pheasants were unfit to kill before this time. Two or three large scale driven shoots might be held prior to Christmas, lasting from two to four days with an expected bag of around 1,000 birds per day. Thereafter, the owner might put on a few walked-up days for local friends or, simply, go out alone in pursuit of the odd pheasant, partridge or hare accompanied by a gamekeeper and a couple of dogs.

Georgian sportsmen pheasant shooting. Coloured etching by Thomas Rowlandson
(after George Morland) 1790

On the smaller, more traditional estates owned by country squires rather than by members of the aristocracy or wealthy businessmen, pheasant and partridge shooting coexisted along with fox hunting. Three or four driven partridge shoots (either residential or non-residential) were usually held in September and October and a similar number of driven pheasant shoots took place in November and December. However, on these properties small mixed walk-up shoots were usually held once or twice a week throughout the season along with a number of dedicated hare and rabbit shoots specifically for the tenant farmers.

Large pheasant bags were the order of the day on all but the smallest shoots. Indeed, in 1913, the last season before the outbreak of World War One, a party of seven Guns headed by King George V took an all-time record bag of 3,937 pheasants at a *battue* held on 18 December at Hall Barn in Buckinghamshire, seat of Lord Burnham (then proprietor of the *Daily Telegraph*). Personal bags, of course, were invariably much bigger. The Marquess of Ripon, for example, one of Britain's top shots, accounted for a total of 5,179 pheasants in 1913 out of a total head of game of 8,233.

Despite the effects of game bird rearing restrictions enacted during both world wars; estate fragmentation, particularly in the wake of World War One; and the many changes in farming methods, forestry and land management that have taken place over the past century or so, the sport of driven pheasant shooting has weathered the storm and continues to be as popular as ever. In fact, the sport has really taken off again over the past forty years or so, fuelled by the rapid growth in commercial driven shoots during this period, many of which specialise in producing high pheasants for discerning paying Guns.

Running a driven pheasant shoot has, of course, always been an expensive business. Indeed, the famous old saying 'up goes a guinea, bang goes a penny halfpenny, and down comes half-a-crown', which refers to the cost of rearing a pheasant, the cost of a cartridge, and the price paid by a game dealer for a dead bird at the end of a shoot is as relevant today as it was in the Edwardian era,

Guns and gamekeepers with members of their families posing for the camera with the day's bag on a mixed walked-up pheasant and rabbit shoot at Trawlers, Dragon's Green, West Sussex 1907: courtesy of the late Captain John Rapley

especially now that it can cost as much as £50 to put a pheasant in the air, with an expected return of between 50p and £1 from the sale of a dead bird.

High pheasants

Seen by many as a product of the late twentieth century, the sport of high pheasant shooting actually dates back to the Victorian period when a number of landowners started to take advantage of valleys, escarpments and other landscape features when laying out drives in order to produce high birds as 'targets' to test the marksmanship abilities of their guests. Estates renowned for high pheasants during the late nineteenth and the early twentieth centuries include Studley Royal in Yorkshire, owned by the celebrated shot, the 2nd Marquess of Ripon; Warter Priory in Yorkshire, seat of Lord Nunburnholme; Stanage Park in Radnorshire, home of Mr C.C.

Shooting driven pheasants at Miltons, Exmoor: courtesy of Roxtons

Rogers; the Worlds End shoot near Llangollen in North Wales (which according to Lord Ashtown 'was probably the finest high bird shoot in the world for very high birds'.); and the Wilton estate in Wiltshire where the Earl of Pembroke's Scottish head keeper, McKellar, 'took a positive delight in bringing birds so high as to beat the Guns' on the famous Groveley beat. High pheasant shooting remained strictly the preserve of the rich and famous until the early 1970s when Wiltshire farmer and commercial shoot operator, David Hitchens, set up the world famous Gurston Down shoot near Salisbury. This was advertised in *The Field* at the time as the 'Highest pheasant and partridge shoot in England', specifically with the aim of providing high birds for paying Guns. Other commercial shoot owners and gamekeepers followed suit over the next decade or so, in particular, Brian Mitchell, now regarded as the father of the Exmoor high bird, who introduced the concept of high pheasant shooting on Exmoor, at Miltons, Chargot, Challacombe and Bulland. He has not only done much to develop modern day high bird gamekeeping and shooting practices, but has also actively promoted the sport both at home and abroad.

The 4th Earl of Kimberley taking a high pheasant watched by his loader and lady c. 1970: courtesy of the GWCT

Red Grouse

Undoubtedly the 'king of game birds', the red grouse is unique to the British Isles and has a shooting season that runs from 12 August – the 'glorious twelfth' – until 10 December. The bird is now confined to northern Midland counties, Northern England, parts of Central and North Wales, parts of Ireland and throughout much of Scotland. Prior to the outbreak of World War Two in 1939, red grouse were present throughout Wales, Scotland (other than the Shetland Islands) and Ireland. Abortive attempts were made to introduce the red grouse into Norfolk and Suffolk during the late nineteenth century. Successful introductions were made on Dartmoor and on Exmoor during the early twentieth century, allowing shooting to take place on a limited scale in the latter region until the early 1970s.

The red grouse has been managed for sporting purposes since the early nineteenth century. Management, however, is carried out through habitat

Male red grouse in winter: courtesy of Lindsay Waddell

Sportsmen walking-up and shooting grouse over dogs. Coloured aquatint by H. Alken 1820

enhancement, vermin eradication and poaching prevention rather than through artificial rearing (although it is possible to rear the birds in captivity). In the late nineteenth and the early twentieth centuries, when labour was plentiful, it was common practice for gamekeepers to provide grit and water supplies on a grouse moor as well as to feed the birds in severe weather by placing stooks of corn at various points on the moor. Red grouse stocks at this time were improved by introducing Scottish birds on to moors in Yorkshire and Lancashire and vice versa, in order to introduce new blood. In North Wales and in Yorkshire, a number of small moors were operated specifically for grouse production, whereby mature birds were netted on a regular basis and supplied to landowners whose stocks had become depleted due to overshooting. In 1913, red grouse could be purchased from Yorkshire dealers for 30/- (£1.50) per brace, a brace in this instance consisting of two hens and a cock.

Considered by many to be the 'rich man's game bird', the red grouse has been walked-up and shot over dogs since Stuart times. Grouse shooting, however, did not really become fashionable amongst the aristocracy and the gentry until the early years of the nineteenth century. At this time some of the more intrepid sportsmen of the day began to undertake shooting expeditions to the English, Welsh and Scottish moors, travelling to their destinations by carriage or on horseback over the new turnpike roads and staying at inns or farmhouses.

Walked-up grouse shooting at this time was not for the faint hearted, as Henry Alken points out in *The National Sports of Great Britain*, published in 1821:

> 'Grouse lie best in fine weather, and may, in the early season, be followed from eight o'clock in the morning, as long as day-light lasts, provided the stamina and inclination of the Gunner last also. A good refreshment at mid-day will forward this. Late in the autumn, from ten to two or three o'clock, is the longest shooting day. Large shot, and the heaviest gun a man can conveniently carry, will be found most effective, as the birds will run to a great distance. Sportsmen generally try to kill the old cock, which runs cackling away, in order to deceive and lead the pursuers from the brood. The cock being dead, the pack will lie until the dogs run upon them.'

Grouse driving

Sportsmen experimented with grouse driving during the early years of the nineteenth century as a means of securing larger bags – grouse driving of some description, apparently, took place on the Bishop of Durham's moor at Horsley as early as 1803 – but the practice was not widely adopted until the Victorian period. Contemporary estate records indicate that driven grouse shooting had started to take place on the Duke of Rutland's moors at Longshaw in Derbyshire in 1849 and was being carried out on a regular basis on the Duke of Devonshire's moors at Bolton Abbey in Yorkshire by the late 1850s. Driving had become commonplace on many of the moors in Yorkshire and Co. Durham by the 1870s and was introduced on the Lowther estate in Westmorland by the Earl of Lonsdale in 1876. By the 1890s, driven grouse shooting had become the principal mode of killing grouse on all of the larger moors in England, Wales and Scotland and on many of the smaller moors, too.

Grouse shooting on a large scale really began from the 1870s onwards, with ever increasing annual bags culminating in a record for the period when eight Guns brought down 9,929 birds on the Earl of Sefton's Abbeystead estate in

Shooting driven grouse from a butt on Ramsgill Moor, North Yorkshire 1934. Butts were originally known as 'batteries'

Lancashire on 12 August 1915. The development of grouse shooting as a sport was helped immensely by the extension of the railway system to the north of England and Scotland, thus making it possible to travel from London and the south of England to the north in hours instead of days. Indeed, by the early years of the twentieth century fast railway connections between sea ports such as Southampton, Liverpool and Tilbury and the moors enabled American millionaires and Indian princes and maharajas to visit Great Britain by transatlantic liner or the weekly Indian Mail Service from Bombay. Some of them came on an annual basis in order to shoot grouse.

Line of grouse butts on the Raby estate Co. Durham: courtesy of Lindsay Waddell. Guns and their loaders are just visible standing in the butts

Pheasant and partridge shooting tended to be the preserve of the shoot owner and his invited guests rather than paying clients until the 1970s. Grouse shooting, on the other hand, was commercialised during the mid-nineteenth century with English and Welsh landowners letting out their moors to wealthy businessmen or members of the aristocracy and the landed gentry either annually or for a month or a fortnight at a time. It was something of a tradition on some northern moors for the owner to let the shooting from 12 August until the end of September or early October at a relatively high rental and to retain the remainder of the season for his own use. Accommodation for paying Guns was either provided in a specially built shooting lodge (often referred to as a 'shooting box') or in a local inn or farmhouse dependent upon the size of the moor.

Grouse shooting party taking an 'elevenses stop' on the Raby estate Co. Durham: courtesy of Lindsay Waddell

The demand for grouse shooting from British and overseas paying Guns remains buoyant at the present time and the sport not only generates a significant income which benefits many rural communities, but also makes an immense contribution to wildlife habitat management in moorland areas. Grouse shooting is now generally sold by the day rather than for a week or a month at a time but has become more accessible to the less well-off sportsman, many of whom are able to afford the occasional walked-up day towards the end of the season. Moorland proprietors, of course, continue to invest heavily in their grouse moors, employing gamekeepers and estate workers to manage the land in the best interests of grouse preservation and nature conservation, whether or not they run a commercial or a private shoot operation.

THE GROUSE SHOOTER'S NECESSITIES

In his classic work *The Oakleigh Shooting Code*, published in 1836, Thomas Oakleigh lists what he considers to be essential items for a sportsman to take with him when going grouse shooting:

'Dogs; fowling piece, in case or bag; two extra pivots; a pivot pricker; pivot wrench; gun-rod or cleaner; a small bottle of olive oil; some linen-cloth and leather; powder flask; dram-flask; shot belt; bird-bag; a canister of powder; a quantity of shot, various sizes; a few pairs of woollen stockings; strong laced boots; or strong shoes and gaiters; dark shooting dress; copper caps and box; wadding; screw turner; spring cramp; a punch for cutting waddings; shoe oil; straps; collars, couples, and cords for leading and tying up dogs; dog-whistle; dog whip; a pocket comb; some cord or string for tying up game; hampers, in which grouse may be packed between layers of heath; sealing-wax, and seal to mark birds when sent by coach or carrier; game certificate; card of permission, or other authority to produce to the gamekeepers; sandwiches; cigars; soda-powders; prometheans (primitive matches); brandy.'

Woodcock

Revered as a sporting bird, the mysterious and often elusive woodcock has been netted, hawked and shot for centuries. Both a resident and a migrant species, the woodcock is particularly common in south-west Cornwall, the Isles of Scilly and parts of Norfolk and Wales, but can be found in varying numbers in most English and Welsh counties. In England, Wales and Northern Ireland, the woodcock shooting season runs from 1 October to 31 January, and in Scotland from 1 September to 31 January.

Sportsmen walked-up and shot woodcock over dogs until the nineteenth century when driven shooting was introduced on a number of estates. Special coverts of birch, alder, black withy and hazel were planted on these properties in order to attract woodcock. Melton Constable, Sandringham and Holkham in Norfolk and Lanarth in Cornwall were all noted driven woodcock shoots at this time. Record driven woodcock bags include 105 'cock shot in one day in 1860 at Swanton wood at Melton Constable and 106 killed by a team of seven Guns at Lanarth on 21 December 1920.

Woodcock shooting party at Baronscourt, Co. Tyrone, Northern Ireland: courtesy of Abercorn Estates/ www.barons-court.com

Bag of woodcock taken in a day's shooting on a Cornish estate, January 1985: courtesy of the GWCT

Since the outbreak of World War One in 1914, woodcock have generally constituted a part of the bag on a 'mixed day' or as a 'by quarry' on a driven pheasant shoot or an evening flighting expedition. Dedicated driven woodcock shoots, or 'cock shoots as they are more commonly known, are now few and far between in England and Wales other than in Cornwall and on the Isles of Scilly.

Still a much sought after game bird at the present time, the woodcock continues to be regarded as a testing quarry. Indeed, since 1949 any sportsman achieving a right and a left at woodcock can apply, with statements from two witnesses, to join the exclusive *Shooting Times* Woodcock Club.

Wildfowling

The sport of wildfowling is steeped in history. From the medieval period onwards, men living near estuaries, saltings, fens and inland waters and wetland areas went out in pursuit of ducks, geese and waders with nets for food procurement purposes. Over the course of time, fowlers augmented netting by

Wildfowler shooting with a punt mounted gun: courtesy of the GWCT

using primitive shotguns to take their quarry. Unlike game bird shooting, which was regulated by law and restricted to the very rich, wildfowling was something of a cottage industry. For centuries it was carried out by working countrymen either to provide meat for the table or for sales to market traders or itinerant dealers.

Advertisement for a Greener duck shooting gun 1914

Sportsmen started to take an interest in wildfowling during the early nineteenth century, attracted by the challenge of high flying and difficult target birds. The sport gradually increased in popularity and by the mid-Victorian period a considerable number of wealthy shooting enthusiasts were spending the winter months at 'fowling stations' in East Anglia and elsewhere in order to kill various species of wildfowl, shooting with flintlock fowling pieces, large bore shot guns or punt mounted guns, if in a coastal location, and using professional fowlers as guides. Often ex-servicemen, they happily endured cold, wet, and windy conditions, going out at dawn and dusk when 'flighting' for their quarry. They stayed in primitive huts or houseboats for days on end, sleeping in bunks and dining on simple fare.

In 1908, Stanley Duncan, a keen amateur wildfowler and naturalist, formed the Wildfowlers Association of Great Britain and Ireland (WAGBI) in order to protect the interests of fowlers, both professional and amateur, and to conserve wildfowl habitats. The first local association in England, the Southport & District Wildfowlers Association, had actually been established in 1887. Over the next half century or so, a large number of local wildfowling associations and clubs were set up for the same reasons, many of which consisted mainly of working men who could not afford to go shooting on sporting estates. In addition to providing wildfowling and social facilities for their members, most associations and clubs now lease and manage the fowling rights around estuaries, over foreshores and over marshes and ensure that shooting is carried out in a responsible manner. The great majority of wildfowling associations and clubs are affiliated to the British Association for Shooting and Conservation (BASC), the largest shooting organisation in Great Britain.

WILDFOWLING IN POOLE HARBOUR

Historically an important site for wildfowl, Poole Harbour in Dorset is noted for shelduck, gadwall, goldeneye, pochard, scaup, teal and widgeon, as well as various species of wader including avocet, curlew and grey plover. Wildfowling in the harbour, although undertaken by local people for generations, first began to attract sporting tourists during the early nineteenth century following the publication of various books by Colonel Peter Hawker, the well-known diarist, who regularly visited the harbour to shoot ducks and geese using a punt gun in a flat-bottomed 'Poole Canoe'.

By the 1890s, wildfowling was being carried out in Poole Harbour by numerous 'gentleman Guns' and more than twenty professional fowlers, with over forty gunning punts and canoes, operated during the winter months. The wildfowling tradition continues in the harbour today under the auspices of the Dorset Wildfowlers Association, founded in 1952, which leases most of the foreshore from the Crown Estates and now owns and manages Giggers Island, a six acre haven for wildfowl near the port of Wareham.

Ground Game

Commonly referred to as 'ground game' during the Victorian period, hares and rabbits have been pursued for centuries by sportsmen, gamekeepers and poachers alike, using guns, traps, snares and all manner of illegal 'engines of destruction'. Unlike pheasants, partridges and other game birds which are deemed to be the property of a land-owner or his sporting tenant, hares and rabbits can be shot by a tenant farmer or other occupier of rented land (or an authorised person holding written permission from him) under the terms of the Ground Game Act of 1880. In circumstances where a landowner or a sporting tenant holds the sporting rights over a farm or land rented for other purposes, the occupier enjoys a concurrent right with such persons to shoot hares and rabbits on land under his occupation.

Hare

Unlike the rabbit, generally considered to be a pest rather than a quarry species, the hare has always enjoyed an unusual status. It is shot both for sporting and pest control purposes. Hare shooting was banned by King James I in 1614 in order to conserve stocks for hunting. The ban remained in place until 1807. Thereafter, hares were either shot by sportsmen as part of a mixed bag or by gamekeepers carrying out pest control duties.

Hare: courtesy of David Mason

Sportsmen continued to look upon the hare as something of a 'by quarry' until the early 1840s when Prince Albert introduced the German practice of hare driving (driven hare shooting) into Great Britain. This mode of shooting enabled large hare bags to be taken relatively quickly, and soon became popular amongst members of the aristocracy and the landed gentry, some of whom purchased consignments of live hares from London game dealers or from friends in areas where hares were still plentiful, in order to bolster up stocks after local populations had become depleted.

Overshooting of hares by sportsmen during the 1860s and 1870s, and by tenant farmers and others following the passage of the Ground Game Act in 1880, prompted a number of landowners to set up hare preservation associations during the late nineteenth century to encourage tenants not to destroy hares in order to preserve them for organised shoots. In return for not shooting hares or informing their landlord of any hares that they had inadvertently shot, tenants were rewarded with a share of the bag taken at covert shoots or on hare drives.

Sadly, hare preservation associations were not always effective and in some districts hares had become extremely scarce by the late Edwardian era due to a combination of excessive shooting and over-poaching. Hare populations increased considerably during World War One, when shooting activities were reduced on the great majority of sporting estates, with the result that by the early 1920s hares had become plentiful again in many areas.

Hare shooting remained a popular sport until the mid-twentieth century in districts which continued to support a high population of hares, in particular on Salisbury Plain, the Oxfordshire Downs, the North and South Downs and in parts of North Hampshire and Dorset. Driven hare shoots on farms and estates in these localities were generally large affairs involving between thirty and forty Guns and up to thirty-five beaters, several of whom would act as 'walking Guns'.

Sportsman with a bag of hares c. 1920

As many as eight or ten drives might be held in a day, with an expected bag of between 200 and 400 hares.

In addition to organising driven hare shoots for parties of invited guests, it was something of a tradition for landowners in districts with a high hare population to hold several driven or walked-up hare days for the tenant farmers on their properties every February just after the end of the main shooting season. Usually hosted by the head gamekeeper, who was often allowed to invite gamekeeper friends from adjoining estates to make up Gun numbers, these events were not only something of a social occasion but also ensured that a cordial relationship existed between members of the gamekeeping and the farming fraternity.

Other than in areas where hares continue to be a serious agricultural pest, dedicated hare shoots are held at the end of each game bird shooting season for pest control purposes. Hare shooting has been disbanded on many farms and sporting estates. Indeed, a considerable number of shoot owners now refrain from shooting any hares at all due to the general decline in hare numbers which has occurred over the past fifty years.

Rabbit

Rabbit shooting was an extremely popular activity during the Victorian period when the rabbit was a major agricultural pest throughout much of Great Britain. Rabbits were, in fact, preserved for sporting purposes on many country estates at this time, sometimes in specially constructed warrens. The rabbit was also introduced into a number of rabbit-less districts for sport during the nineteenth century, including the Lizard Peninsula in Cornwall and parts of Ross-shire in Scotland. Dedicated driven shoots were regularly held during February and March to prevent rabbits from eating young crops. Large numbers were shot on a daily basis, with exceptionally high bags being attained. For example, at Blenheim Palace in Oxfordshire a total of 6,943 rabbits were killed by a team of five Guns on 7 October 1898.

Large scale driven rabbit shoots continued to be held on some sporting estates until the 1920s and '30s, particularly on properties where the bulk of

Sportsmen and their ladies posing for the camera during the lunch break on a rabbit shoot at Dufton, Westmorland 1913

the land was farmed in-hand rather than tenanted. Thereafter, rabbit shooting seems to have gone out of favour amongst the aristocracy and the gentry and became very much the sport of farmers, shooting syndicates, working men and members of the poaching fraternity.

Many landowners, however, scaled down driven rabbit shooting operations on their property following the passage of the Ground Game Act of 1880 – which gave tenant farmers and others the right to kill rabbits and hares on rented land under their occupation. In these circumstances, walked-up rabbit shooting continued to be carried out on a regular basis over in-hand land by sportsmen and gamekeepers, both for sport and pest control, with, perhaps two or three driven days being held during the course of the season, together with a 'keepers' day' after Christmas for the benefit of the gamekeeping staff and their friends.

Some of the gentleman farming tenants who rented large areas of prime agricultural land in East Anglia, the Midlands and parts of the south of England took full advantage of the Ground Game Act and regularly held organised rabbit shoots and hare drives. However, the great majority of tenant farmers generally trapped or snared rabbits rather than shot at them, other than at harvest time when special 'harvest shoots' were arranged to cull rabbits as the corn was being cut in the fields by a reaper and binder. Such 'harvest shoots' were something of a social occasion during the late nineteenth and the first half of the twentieth centuries, with neighbouring farmers and local gamekeepers participating and a substantial meal being provided at the end of the day.

Since the arrival of myxomatosis in Great Britain in 1953, which decimated rabbit populations throughout the country, the rabbit has become very much the preserve of the rough shooter and the gamekeeper or forms part of the bag on a 'mixed day'. Sadly, like the hare, the rabbit has become increasingly scarce in recent years and is now on the verge of extinction in some areas.

Richard Lloyd-Price – the 'Rabbit King'

Considered to be the greatest expert on rabbit shooting in Britain during the late Victorian period, Richard John Lloyd-Price, an eccentric Welsh squire nicknamed 'The Rabbit King', was born posthumously in 1843. While still at college in Oxford, he inherited the vast Rhiwlas estate near Bala in North Wales upon the death of his grandfather, Richard Watkin Price, in 1860.

A keen sportsman, Richard gradually turned the Rhiwlas estate into a vast game preserve, employing a team of six gamekeepers and establishing a driven pheasant shoot on the property that was capable of producing extremely high birds. He also introduced organised grouse shooting on Rhiwlas Moor, managing the ground so well that an annual bag of up to 1,000 brace was attainable in a good season.

However, Richard was principally interested in developing large scale driven rabbit shooting at Rhiwlas, a sport which he felt could become a lucrative activity for estate owners and farmers. He laid out a giant 'rabbit park' on the property, by erecting a wire fence around a small mountain and constructing artificial warrens inside the boundary. In addition to the existing rabbit stock on the ground, he put down consignments of live rabbits brought in from other estates to improve the existing blood, and advocated regular introductions of rabbits from elsewhere to avoid degeneration and disease amongst the inhabitants of his warrens.

Richard established a rabbit breeding station at Rhiwlas to provide a constant supply of young rabbits for his warrens and pioneered the use of artificial incubators for rearing purposes. For shooting, he recommended wild rabbits only, but for food production suggested that the most suitable rabbit was a cross between a wild rabbit and a Belgian hare.

Keen to promote rabbit preservation both for sporting purposes and as a means of making money through the sale of rabbits to poulterers and butchers in manufacturing towns, Richard wrote numerous articles advocating the benefits of 'rabbit farming' in *The Field* and other sporting papers. He frequently told his readers that whereas a cow consumes the same amount of grass daily as 150 rabbits, the profit made from a cow over twelve weeks amounted to £6, while the profit made from 150 rabbits over the same period totalled £11/5/0 (£11.25).

Richard gradually developed a system of driven rabbit shooting which would produce large daily bags for parties of between seven and ten Guns. He implemented specialist hole blocking techniques that included the use of paraffin, to keep rabbits out on the ground in readiness for a shoot day. He employed teams of beaters to drive rabbits towards the Guns on the day. His shoot accounts for 1883 reveal that he paid a gamekeeper a yearly salary of £52 to look after his warrens and spent £4/8/0 (£4.40) on casual labour for hole blocking, beating and ferreting.

Richard spent many years building up his driven rabbit shoot at Rhiwlas, and established a team of eight other Guns comprising Lord Abinger, Earl de Grey, the Duke of Hamilton, Lord Berkeley Paget, James Pender, C. Wilson, R. Rimington-Wilson and W.R.M. Wynne. The team killed a record daily bag of 5,096 rabbits on Rhiwlas warren on 7 October 1885 – Earl de Grey alone accounting for 920 rabbits. Other notable bags taken on the property included 3,660 rabbits shot by seven Guns on 16 October 1884, and 3,093 taken by eight Guns on 19 October 1887.

Unlike many of his neighbours, who ran shoots for the benefit of their family and friends, Richard introduced sporting lets at Rhiwlas, enabling wealthy businessmen to shoot on his land on a 'paying guest' basis. This was a practice that did not go down very well with his farming tenants. In addition, keen to capitalise upon the growing popularity of shooting, he established Rhiwlas Game Farm which supplied landowners with pheasant eggs, live hares and rabbits for stocking purposes.

Farmers out rabbit shooting at harvest time c. 1910

Nominated by *Baily's* magazine as one of the sixty best shots in Great Britain, Richard received many invitations to shoot on famous estates during the late Victorian and Edwardian periods. He even managed to visit the 69,000 acre Park Deer Forest on the remote island of Lewis in the Outer Hebrides in 1874 as the guest of the lessee, Frank Hemming. He enjoyed superlative deer stalking, walked-up grouse shooting and sea trout fishing on the property.

When not shooting rabbits and other game, Richard was actively involved in horse racing and owned a number of prize winning racehorses. He was an avid dog lover, too, and kept a kennel of over one hundred dogs, ranging from pointers to bull terriers. Keen on breed improvement, he exhibited his gun dogs at field trials and established sheepdog trials at Garth Goch near Bala in 1873 for the benefit of local farmers and shepherds.

In addition to his many sporting interests, Richard found time to establish various industries on the Rhiwlas estate ranging from a brick works and a saw mill to a soap factory and a whisky distillery. He also wrote a number of fieldsports related books including *Practical Pheasant Rearing*, *Dogs Ancient and Modern* and *Rabbits for Profit and Rabbits for Powder*.

After a long and productive life, Richard Lloyd-Price, the 'Rabbit King', died on 9 January 1923, at the ripe old age of eighty years. He was laid to rest in a vault in Llanfor Cemetery which he had built in 1887 with money won by his racehorse, Bendigo. The inscription on the vault reads 'As to my latter end I go, to meet my jubilee, I thank my good horse Bendigo, who built this tomb for me.'

GAME PRESERVATION, GAME PROTECTION AND GAME SHOOTING ASSOCIATIONS

Poaching was rife throughout much of England and Wales during the mid-eighteenth century, in part due to a legal regulation which prevented a lord of the manor from employing more than one gamekeeper on his property. In an effort to combat the theft of game on manorial and other estates, groups of noblemen and squires began to form associations for the preservation of game. These organisations offered substantial rewards to any member of the public who acted as an informant on poaching activities, following the successful prosecution of offenders. For example, The Association for the Preservation of Game all over England, a national body set up in 1752 by a group of leading landowners, offered a flat fee of £5 for a wide variety of offences including illegally killing and taking hares, pheasants, partridges, black game or red grouse; successfully convicting a gamekeeper for killing or selling game without the consent of his master; and for successfully convicting an 'unqualified' person such as a stage-coachman, a poulterer or an innkeeper for buying and selling game.

Other contemporary game preservation associations offered a variable scale of rewards, ranging from £1 for reporting illegal fishing activities to £10 for providing evidence which resulted in the successful prosecution of night poachers. Although these payments were extremely generous,

---

INSTRUCTIONS

FOR THE

USE OF THE MEMBERS OF THE ASSOCIATION

THEIR GAMEKEEPERS AND OTHERS.

The objects of the Association being the protection of Game in the County of Hants, the prevention of the illicit sale of Eggs, to prevent as far as possible trepasses in pursuit of Game, night poaching, and other offences under the Game Laws, and to punish offenders against such Laws, it is necessary that each Member faithfully and firmly discharges his duty to further the objects of the Association, *giving information forthwith to the Secretary* of all trespassers and poachers found on the lands of any of the Members of the Association, or over which they have the right of sporting, and of all offences which may come to their knowledge, with a view to bringing such offenders to justice, and thus to put a stop as far as possible to the repetition of such offences, to protect Game, and to prevent the damage in many instances sustained by tenants to fences, gates, &c., by trespassers in pursuit of Game, &c.

No Member shall purchase Partridge Eggs, English or Foreign, without immediately informing the Secretary of his source of supply.

Each Member shall buy, in preference, Pheasants' Eggs from Farms that are sanctioned by the Association, and if a Member purchases Eggs from other Game Farmers he shall inform the Secretary of the fact.

No Member shall buy Pheasants' Eggs of any person, who, having no land of his own, has to buy from other persons to sell again.

Instructions supplied to members of the Hampshire Game Protection Association 1902

especially when farm workers were paid around 8/- (40p) a week, it is on record that few people came forward with information, possibly out of fear of recrimination or because they enjoyed the odd rabbit 'for the pot' given to them by a less than honest friend or neighbour.

Game preservation associations continued to act as a deterrent against poaching until the mid-1850s when many were disbanded due to the establishment of the county police forces. Those that remained often turned their attention to stopping supply lines of stolen game from the country to big cities – usually stage coaches, canal barges or trains where the guard had been bribed by a poaching gang to pick up sealed hampers of rabbits, pheasants or other game at a prearranged point such as a signal stop.

The rapid increase in the sport of shooting in the late Victorian and the Edwardian periods led to the formation of a number of new organisations, known as game protection associations, that were not only interested in prosecuting poachers but also suppressing the illegal trafficking of pheasant and partridge eggs. Such associations were set up in Ireland (1891), East Anglia (early 1890s), Essex (1897), Hampshire (1902) and Bedfordshire (1904). In addition, a body known as the Game Guild was founded by a group of influential landowners to inspect game farms and to 'police' the importation of partridges and partridge eggs from Hungary and other Central European countries.

Few game protection associations appear to have survived beyond the 1920s. Notable exceptions being the East Anglian Game Protection Society (disbanded around 1990) and the Essex Game Guild, which was re-formed as a shooting and countrysports club in 1955 and currently has in excess of 150 members.

Since the 1950s, a number of game shooting associations have been established in various parts of England to protect the interests of local shooters as well as to combat poaching activities. The West Sussex Game Shooting Association, founded in 1957 but now disbanded, also organised an annual vermin killing competition, awarding prizes to full- and part-time gamekeepers based on the number of 'heads' or 'tails' killed. It also held a series of winter film shows and lectures for its members. Present day shooting associations include the Tamar Valley Shooting and Conservation Association and the Greater Exmoor Shoots Association, both of which also promote game shooting in the West Country.

SHOOTING IN
SCOTLAND

GAME SHOOTING FOR SPORTING PURPOSES has been carried out in Scotland since the late sixteenth century, although it appears to have been confined very much to the southern and central parts of the country until the late eighteenth century when the first intrepid English sportsmen began to make the long journey north to the Highlands in pursuit of grouse, salmon and stags. Accompanied by rod, gun and a brace of pointers or setters, these men arrived

Shooting party at Achany, Sutherland 1890: courtesy of Sir Andrew de la Rue, Bt. Back row, left to right: Lady Matheson of the Lews, Mrs Perceval, Master Cecil Hunter. Front row, left to right: George Waring, Mr Hunter, Edward Sanford. Achany gamekeeper, Mr Campbell sits in front of the Guns with dogs Rufus and Dinah

by stagecoach or boat, or a combination of both, and happily endured spartan living conditions in a primitive inn or a crofter's cottage in order to shoot and fish over large tracts of land for weeks or months on end. They paid the local laird little or nothing for the privilege as game in the Highlands was so abundant and considered to be of little value at the time.

Encouraged by the activities of these English sportsmen, Highland lairds began to take up game shooting themselves during the early years of the nineteenth century. The more canny amongst them, especially those who had become impoverished through living the 'high life' in London, realised that money could be made from shootings and fishings. They started to let out the sporting rights on their properties to Englishmen, a practice which had become increasingly common by the 1820s and '30s. Indeed, in 1834, *Anderson's Guide to the Highlands and Islands of Scotland* observed that 'Moors may be had at all prices from £50 to £500 (over £22,000 in today's prices) for the season, with accommodation varying according to circumstances.'

However, the first formal letting agreements did not come into being until 1836 when Hugh Snowie, an enterprising Inverness gunmaker, set up Scotland's first sporting agency and published a list offering eight shootings for rental. Something of an entrepreneur, Mr Snowie also hired out pointers and setters, provided seasonal gamekeepers and ghillies on an agency basis, and employed a taxidermist for preserving 'trophy' birds or heads shot by his clients.

SHOOTING

'To let, for such a term of years as may be agreed on, THE RIGHT of SHOOTING over the Estate of ALDOURIE and BALNAIN, parish of Dores, County of Inverness. The Winter Shooting on these Grounds, which extend for 10 miles along the Banks of Lochness, is equal to any in Britain. The abundance of Woodcocks is so great that from 50 to 100 Couple may be flushed in a forenoon beat, by three guns and three beaters. The Grounds abound also with Roe Deer and Black Game, besides Hares, Partridges and Grouse – and there are numerous Lakes on the Property affording excellent Trout and Pike Fishing. There is regular communication by Steam both to the east and the west sea.'

Apply to the Proprietor,
WM. Fraser Tytler, Esq., Sanquhar House, Forres
15th March 1830

The Reverend George Hely-Hutchinson (on far left with fishing creel on back and game carrier in hand), an early Highland sporting tenant with a group of friends c. 1860. Rector of Westport St. Mary with Brokenborough and Charlton in Wiltshire from 1837 until 1876, the Reverend Hely-Hutchinson rented various shootings in Ross-shire during the 1830s and '40s and leased the 75,000 acre Soval estate on the island of Lewis from 1852 to 1869

Throughout the late 1830s and the 1840s an ever increasing number of sportsmen began to visit Scotland for the shooting season. While minor members of the landed gentry and former army officers were quite happy to 'rough it' on their journey north, the fashionable aristocrats and wealthy industrialists who came were not only prepared to pay large sums of money for the privilege of shooting grouse or stalking deer, but also wanted to travel to the shooting and fishing in comfort, bringing with them their wives and families along with a retinue of servants. Many took a steam ship from London to Aberdeen or Inverness, a journey that often took six or seven days to accomplish (and usually cost in excess of £15), then continued the journey to their shooting quarters by carriage.

The Royal Example

The shooting industry really began to take off in Scotland from the early 1850s onwards after Queen Victoria and Prince Albert inadvertently popularised 'sporting tourism' through acquiring the Balmoral estate on Deeside in 1848, making it fashionable for the rich and famous in society to either rent or lease a Scottish sporting property for the season. Landowners throughout the country, from the Border counties to the Orkney and Shetland islands, started to let out shootings and fishings in order to satisfy the demand for grouse moors, deer forests and salmon rivers from wealthy southern tenants, spurred on by the rapidly expanding rail network which enabled tenants to reach all but the most remote districts from London within the space of twenty-four hours. Quick to capitalise on this demand, Sir James Matheson of the Lews, Bt., an astute businessman but not a sportsman himself, divided up the vast 404,000 acre Lewis estate in the Outer Hebrides. He formed a total of twelve sporting subjects for rental purposes, on land formerly used for sheep farming, between 1850 and the time of his death in 1878. He created mixed shootings, fisheries and deer forests with associated lodges and recruited a team of thirty gamekeepers to

Balmoral Castle, shooting quarters for the Balmoral estate. The castle was rebuilt in its present form in 1853 by Queen Victoria and Prince Albert

manage his sporting portfolio, along with a vast number of seasonally employed ghillies and river watchers. Other major Highland landowners followed suit, converting large scale sheep farms into 'general shootings' or deer forests during the period 1850 to 1890.

Scottish landowners, of course, spent large sums of money developing shootings and deer forests throughout the second half of the nineteenth century. They built commodious lodges to accommodate their clients, constructed good access roads and stalking tracks, erected deer fences and provided yacht mooring facilities for sporting tenants if in a coastal location. Some also attempted to improve local game stocks by putting down red deer stags from English deer parks in their deer forests and red grouse from Yorkshire and elsewhere on their moors, and provided small scale pheasant and partridge shoots for the benefit of tenants in climatically unsuitable places by annually importing consignments of birds from game farms. Obviously keen to optimise the income from such heavy investment, many landowners not only offered main season shootings for red deer stags, grouse and other game commencing on 4 August and finishing on 10 November, but also provided winter shootings for red deer hinds, wildfowl and woodcock, beginning on 15 November and ending on 28 February.

Above: *Morsgail, one of an assortment of shooting lodges built on the Lewis estate by Sir James Matheson, Bt.*

Left: *Sir James Matheson, Bt., an astute businessman who converted the large sheep farms on the Lewis estate into sporting subjects for letting purposes*

Sporting Tenants

Sporting tenants at this time generally had access to a far wider range of game quarry species on a Scottish property than on an average English or Welsh estate. For example, the 6,000 acre Abercairney estate in Perthshire (which consisted of 3,300 acres of low ground, 2,000 acres of moorland and 700 acres of woodland) offered deer, red grouse, capercailzie, black game, pheasants, partridges, wild duck, woodcock, snipe, pigeons, brown hares, blue hares, rabbits and 'various', plus loch fishing for brown and Loch Leven trout. Highland properties invariably provided ptarmigan shooting, red deer stalking and salmon and sea trout fishing, while those situated on the coast might offer seal shooting and the possibility of participating in a whale hunt. Game books kept by the sportsmen of the day indicate that some shot at just about everything in sight, as entries often include the odd heron, snow bunting, corncrake, curlew, dotterel and the occasional golden eagle.

Shooting party with the day's bag on the Dundonnell estate, Ross-shire c. 1870

SEAL SHOOTING

Seals have been culled around the coast Scotland for several centuries in order to prevent them causing too much damage to salmon stocks. During the late Victorian period seal destruction was regarded as a form of sport and sportsmen often went out seal clubbing or shooting when not engaged in the pursuit of grouse or deer. Various reports of sealing expeditions survive. For example in November 1897, after a large number of seals had been sighted in the vicinity of the island of North Rona, forty miles north of the Butt of Lewis on the island of Lewis. The *Inverness Courier* noted:

'Last week an expedition was fitted out for sealing purposes, and from reports now to hand, it would seem that the venture was fairly successful, and that a large number of seals fell to the sportsmen. The boats having returned at the end of last week with part of their spoils, it appears that about 100 seals were landed at the Port of Ness, and on Saturday an additional 86 were brought and landed at Stornoway harbour. The hunting of the seal in North Rona might be recommended as an exciting pastime for adventurous sportsmen. It must present numerous excitements – the dangerous voyage to the uninhabited Island in the far North, the subsequent life in a turf hut, the glorious adventure of the chase – capital antidotes one should say from the ennui of a London Drawing room.'

Seal shoot at Gress, Island of Lewis 1930. Head gamekeeper, John Murdo Macdonald (left) walked along the cliff top playing the bagpipes to attract seals in order that the sporting tenant, Gilbert Holmes (right) could shoot them

Sporting tenant, Sir Frederick Milbank, Bt., (lying down) and his stalking team with a grassed stag at Ardvourlie, Isle of Harris 1865: courtesy of Sir Anthony Milbank, Bt.

Specialist Letting Agents

Shootings, fishings and deer forests were usually let through a specialist agent who charged a commission of five per cent of the rental value of a property (which was normally paid by the proprietor and the sporting tenant in equal proportions) rather than by the landowner or his factor. Scottish sporting properties were advertised in brochures published annually by the principal letting agents such as Robert Hall, who operated The Highland Sportsman Shooting and Estate Agency from offices in Old Bond Street, London; The Club Shooting and Fishing Agency based in Hanover Square, London; Tom Speedy of Edinburgh (a former gamekeeper); and James Watson Lyall of 15 Pall Mall, London. Mr Watson Lyall also produced *The Sportsman's, Tourist's & General Guide to the Rivers, Lochs, Moors & Deer Forests of Scotland*, issued monthly, which was regarded as essential reading for potential sporting tenants as it contained details of landowners, rental and rateable values, river seasons and rail and steamer timetables.

Cover of The Sportsman's, Tourist's & General Guide to the Rivers, Lochs, Moors & Deer Forests of Scotland - *the inside pages of which were invaluable to anyone seeking information connected with fishing, stalking and shooting*

In addition to paying the rent, and sometimes the sporting rates on an estate, a tenant was often obliged to reimburse the proprietor for the wages of the gamekeepers and ghillies during his term of occupation and to compensate him if the game stocks had become depleted through excessive shooting. For example when George Strutt of Makeney House, Derby, rented the Ardkinglas shootings in Argyll from George Callendar for the sum of £1,200 for the 1897 season he was also expected to pay the salary of the head gamekeeper, John Brodie, which amounted to £60; to give a gratuity of £9/10/0 (£9.50) to the local

Guns, gamekeepers and beaters at the end of the day on a Scottish grouse moor c. 1910.
The ponies on the left of the photograph are equipped with grouse carrying panniers

shepherds for keeping a watching brief over the game birds and fish; and to pay an allowance of £1/5/3 (£1.26½) to the district foxhunter for killing any foxes on the property. Mr Strutt's tenancy agreement gave him the exclusive right to kill hares and rabbits at Ardkinglas but restricted the red grouse bag to 350 brace, the black cock bag to 3 brace, and prohibited the shooting of any hinds or hen pheasants. However, he was allowed the use of the estate steam launch and a rowing boat.

The Scottish shooting industry flourished throughout the late Victorian and Edwardian periods, providing well paid employment for gamekeepers, ghillies and domestic staff working in shooting lodges, and giving trade to a variety of local businesses, ranging from grocers and carriage hirers to gunsmiths and taxidermists. In 1900, the estimated annual expenditure by sportsmen on the 3,157 grouse moors and general shootings and 197 deer forests in Scotland was around £1.5 million. This figure had increased to nearly £2 million by 1909. In addition, the Scottish salmon rivers yielded a further income of around £200,000 at this time.

World War One

Sadly, when World War One was declared in 1914, the Scottish shooting industry crashed almost overnight. Large numbers of sporting tenants and gamekeepers joined the armed services, with the result that numerous estates were either mothballed or only very lightly keepered and often heavily poached. Travel restrictions imposed under the Defence of the Realm Act dealt a further blow, preventing elderly tenants from going north to shoot or fish, wherever sporting facilities were still available.

Following the cessation of hostilities in 1918, a large number of Scottish landowners scaled down their land holdings, selling off surplus estates, sections of estates or shooting and fishing rights in order to pay off high tax bills or death duties. Many previously let sporting properties were purchased by English businessmen, often former tenants, for the exclusive use of their families or friends. Instead of being managed by a team of gamekeepers and ghillies, these properties were left in the charge of a single keeper, who often doubled as a shepherd or a shooting lodge caretaker. In some cases, particularly in the Outer Hebrides, some properties became unkeepered crofting estates with rough shootings and fishings, which were usually leased to a local doctor, bank manager or shopkeeper. The letting market for shootings subsequently dipped, with agents concentrating on other areas of business such as property sales or surveying.

John Morrison, a Stornoway businessman rented the unkeepered 35,000 acre Galson shootings on the Isle of Lewis for the 1933 season for the princely sum of £40, but was restricted to a bag limit of 60 brace of grouse

LIFE ON A SCOTTISH SPORTING ESTATE IN THE 1930s

Keith McDougall, a retired Norfolk Farmer, enthusiastic sportsman and extremely talented artist, provides a brief insight into life on a Scottish sporting estate in the late 1930s in his book of landscape paintings, *A Special Kind of Light*:

'I have in my possession the game book for a single season at Cluny Castle on Upper Speyside in Scotland. My parents took the estate and rented it for three months, August to October 1937 in those golden years just before World War Two. A procession of family and friends came to enjoy Highland hospitality at the castle and to range over 10,000 acres of hill and stream. The range of game shot and caught was astonishing. Grouse were walked-up, ptarmigan pursued on the tops, hill lochs fished for trout, stags stalked, pheasants, snipe, partridges, hares, rabbits, duck on the river, often with small expeditions of one or two Guns rambling over the ground and a few formal days. A staggering 2,081 head of game was bagged including 728 grouse and 8 stags. Records show only two keepers on the estate and one or two ghillies in attendance. Photographs in the family album show picnics in the heather, wooden framed shooting brakes parked, ponies at rest and fish laid out by peaty burns – an idyllic scenario of leisure and sport.'

American socialite, Miss Grace Amory shooting grouse on Herbert Pulitzer's hired moor in Perthshire, August 1939. Newspaper magnate, Mr Pulitzer was one of a number of wealthy Americans to rent Scottish shootings during the 1920s and '30s

Other than on large, prestigious sporting properties where wealthy landowners continued to run private shoots for the benefit of their family and friends or were able to let out deer stalking, grouse and salmon fishing to 'blue chip' British and American clients, the Scottish shooting industry became a relatively low key affair in many areas for the next half century or so. Indeed, some of the more enterprising estate owners started offering shooting and stalking for a week or a fortnight at a time rather than on a seasonal basis. They rented out their sporting rights to a local hotelier or resorted to self-letting in an attempt to solicit tenants by placing an advertisement in a sporting periodical such as *The Field* or in a daily paper.

Sporting Tourism in the 1960s

Sporting tourism began to pick up again in the late 1960s, fuelled by a renewed interest in Scottish shooting, fishing and deer stalking by British, European and American sportsmen, many of whom took advantage of air travel or improved road links to reach the estate of their choice rather than the time honoured and more leisurely night sleeper train service from London. Landowners rose to the challenge, revitalising run-down estates and renovating dilapidated shooting lodges to modern day standards. They installed additional bathrooms, central heating and fitted carpets in order to attract wealthy paying guests who preferred home comforts to the dated accommodation that was acceptable to the more traditional tenant.

Since the 1970s, the Scottish shooting industry has gone from strength to strength, attracting large numbers of British and overseas sportsmen to Scotland annually. It makes an extremely valued contribution to the local economy in many rural areas by creating much needed employment and through the purchase of goods and services. Sporting facilities are now widely advertised throughout the world by a small number of specialist agents able to cater for the needs of even the most fastidious clients. They offer weekly or fortnightly lets and can arrange lets of a shorter or longer duration if required. Scottish sporting tourists even have a dedicated magazine the *Scottish Sporting Gazette*, a bi-annual publication that keeps visitors informed about the latest developments in shooting, fishing and deer stalking throughout Scotland.

Doing the Highland Circuit

The golden age of the Scottish shooting industry lasted from the late 1870s until the outbreak of World War One in 1914. During this era a small group of wealthy sportsmen made an annual pilgrimage to the Highlands of Scotland in pursuit of grouse, salmon and stags, renting a different sporting estate or deer forest annually, or taking a property on a short lease for a term of three or seven years. Many of these men 'did the circuit' of the principal estates in Ross-shire, Sutherland, Inverness-shire and the Outer Hebrides over a period of several decades, not only shooting, fishing and stalking as dedicated sporting tenants but on properties rented by friends or as invited guests of local landowners.

The bulk of these sportsmen were highly successful London businessmen and professionals who had amassed large sums of money in the metropolis during the late Victorian period, either in industry, the law, accountancy, banking or on the Stock Exchange. They often lived in modest houses, did not own a country estate and were relatively unknown in 'society' other than in a professional capacity. A small minority were men of independent means, Indian maharajas or American millionaires on a long term visit to Britain, or minor English landowners and impoverished 'sprigs' of the aristocracy who could not afford to purchase their own Highland sporting property.

Grouse shooting party on a Highland estate c. 1900. The Guns are in the front row;
the gamekeepers are sat at the rear

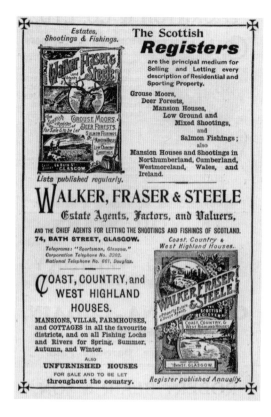

Advertisement for Walker, Fraser & Steele of Glasgow, one of the principal Scottish letting agents 1904

During the long winter evenings each year, these Highland sporting enthusiasts would pour through the letting brochures issued by James Watson Lyall & Co. of Pall Mall, London; The Highland Sporting Shooting & Estate Agency of Old Bond Street, London; Walker, Fraser & Steele of Glasgow; and other smaller sporting agents in order to select an estate or deer forest to rent the following season, often following recommendations made by friends. The ultra-wealthy amongst them might choose a large deer forest, complete with a grouse moor, productive salmon fishings and a large shooting lodge, while the more cost conscious would look for a mixed shooting in a relatively remote location which might offer walked-up grouse, a few salmon and the odd stag.

Highland estate rentals varied immensely at this time, according to the size and quality of the accommodation, accessibility by road and rail, the availability of a safe yacht anchorage and last but not least, bag limits imposed by a landowner and his factor. For example, in 1901, a sporting tenant could expect to pay from £5,000 per annum (£285,300 in today's prices) for a top mainland deer forest to around £120 (£7,000 today) for a large 20,000 acre Outer Hebridean estate. Grouse at this time were stated to be worth between £1/10/0 (£1.50) and £1/15/0 (£1.75) per brace, stags from £20 to £30 each and salmon from £2 to £10 per fish.

Having secured the sporting property of his choice from the letting agent early in the New Year, a sportsman on the 'Highland Circuit' could concentrate wholeheartedly upon his business affairs in the city until the end of July. He would then travel north to the Highlands by train in a specially reserved compartment on the night sleeper from Kings Cross to Scotland. He would pick up a chartered steam yacht at a west coast port or a horse drawn carriage at the nearest railhead to take him to his ultimate destination, often a commodious shooting lodge equipped with the latest 'mod cons'. He would entrust the day to day running of his business to a capable chief clerk, who would often keep in touch with him on a daily basis by letter, telegraph or primitive telephone.

Upon arrival at his Highland estate, a 'Circuit' sportsman and his party, usually his family and a couple of friends, along with their respective servants, would settle down in the shooting lodge and await 12 August with keen anticipation. Some men would spend a day or two fishing for salmon or trout to pass the time while others would simply relax, play cards or go for long walks. Thereafter,

Inverlael Lodge, Lochbroom, Ross-shire c. 1910, Inverlael was one of the many shooting lodges built throughout the Highlands during the late Victorian period to accommodate sportsmen. Tenants not only had the use of a 15,000 acre deer forest (said to be capable of yielding 40 to 50 stags and 20 hinds annually) and 6,000 acres of moorland shooting for red grouse, ptarmigan, woodcock and other game, but also benefited from 1½ miles of single-bank fishing for salmon and sea trout on the river Broom

Family group relaxing in the grounds of a Highland shooting lodge 1890

the party would be out on the moor, hill or river in pursuit of grouse, stags, salmon and other quarry on alternate days, usually on every day of the week except for the Sabbath. Any 'trophy' stag heads taken or large salmon landed during the course of their stay would be despatched to a taxidermist in Inverness for preservation, eventually to grace the hall or dining room in their London home as a memento of the chase.

Prior to returning to England at the end of the season, sportsmen on the 'Highland Circuit' would invariably organise a 'Ghillies Ball' for the estate staff, local tradesmen and others who had contributed to the success of their sojourn. In addition to providing a ball and dinner, some would also put on a fishing competition for the keepers and ghillies – the winners were awarded cash prizes. They also gave a substantial sum of money for the benefit of the poor in the district, food parcels to the sick and elderly and paid for a sumptuous tea for the children at the local school.

George Maclean
from
H N Dugmore

in remembrance of 1898 at
Scaliscro:.

Inscription in a copy of Shooting: Moor And Marsh *presented by H.N. Dugmore, sporting tenant of the Scaliscro estate on the island of Lewis, to George Maclean, the estate gamekeeper*

A surprising number of the men who did the 'Highland Circuit' were first generation sportsmen whose experience of gunnery had initially been gained while serving with London territorial regiments. Nevertheless, they took lessons at London shooting schools, which was something frowned upon by the aristocracy and landed gentry, and ultimately became highly successful marksmen under the tutelage of Highland gamekeepers, who often became lifelong friends. Many picked up their angling skills from Highland keepers and ghillies, too, rather than from the casting experts at Farlow's, Hardy's and other prestigious establishments.

Ghillies enjoying a joke with a sportsman at Glen Muick 1910

Gentlemen and professional deer stalkers, and ghillies posing for the camera in a Highland deer forest 1890

From the London professional classes, members of the Stock Exchange were particularly well represented on the 'Highland Circuit'. Walter Parrott was typical of these men. An independent stockbroker, born in 1857 and married to a rich American heiress, he rented various deer forests and estates annually from the late 1880s until the outbreak of World War One in 1914, including Galson, Grimersta, Morsgail and Lews Castle on the Isle of Lewis, Corriemony in Inverness-shire, Breamore in Ross-shire, ultimately taking a seven-year lease on the 14,000 acre Barrisdale Deer Forest in Inverness-shire, where he grassed a 'royal' that was claimed to be the best head shot in Scotland in 1908.

The legal profession came a close second to the London Stock Exchange on

Bringing home stags at Amhuinnsuidhe, Isle of Harris c. 1920

the 'Highland Circuit' with a number of big names making annual visits to Scotland, including Sir John Rigby, QC, MP, sometime Solicitor-General; William Bailward and Charles Churchill Branch, both top barristers; Francis Lawson and Radclyffe Walters, both prominent solicitors; and William Danckwerts, KC. The latter was a freeman of the City of London and a leading barrister, who specialised in the law pertaining to sporting rights in land valuation cases. He rented a wide variety of sporting subjects, ranging from the shootings and fishings over the entire island of North Uist in the Outer Hebrides to the prestigious 30,000 acre Dundonnell Deer Forest in Ross-shire, and a number of salmon beats on the river Naver in Sutherland.

HIGHLAND GAME

The Highlands of Scotland have long been celebrated for the superb angling, shooting and stalking experiences which they offer to the discerning sportsman. Yet many of the quarry species now found on the estates and deer forests in the region were either introduced within the past two hundred years or so, or improved through the introduction of fresh stock imported from England and other European countries.

PHEASANT

Pheasants were first put down in the Highlands during the mid-nineteenth century when top landowners such as the Duke of Sutherland sent consignments of the birds from his English estate at Lilleshall in Shropshire to Dunrobin Castle in Sutherland in order to establish a pheasant shoot. Other lairds followed suit, purchasing pheasants from London dealers or acquiring them from English friends. Inevitably, some pheasant introduction experiments were doomed to failure, especially in places such as the Isle of Rhum or at Lews Castle in the Outer Hebrides, where a population could only be maintained for sporting purposes by importing new stocks of the birds every year.

PARTRIDGE

The grey partridge has always been present in many parts of the Highlands, albeit in small numbers in some areas. However, in the late nineteenth century native stocks were increased on several estates through the regular importation of partridges or partridge eggs from Hungary in order to have enough birds to satisfy the needs of sporting tenants. The French or 'red-legged' partridge was also put down on a number of Highland properties at this time for the same reason.

RABBIT

Even the humble rabbit was introduced into the Highlands for sporting purposes in 1816 when a rich Gloucestershire cloth manufacturer, Mr Wathen, presented a hamper containing twelve English rabbits to his friend, Sir Hector MacKenzie of Gairloch, Bt., who released them on the Conan estate near Dingwall in Ross-shire. This introduction, was, of course, an immediate success, much to the delight of Sir Hector but not to his crofting and farming neighbours.

CAPERCAILZIE

The capercailzie, which had become extinct in the Highlands and other parts of

Scotland by the late eighteenth century was successfully reintroduced in 1837 using a foundation stock of birds imported from Sweden that were put down on the Marquess of Breadalbane's estate at Taymouth Castle. These birds thrived and spread rapidly, soon providing superlative sport for lairds and their tenants.

RED GROUSE

Throughout the late Victorian and Edwardian periods, thousands of red grouse were imported annually from Yorkshire and put down on many Highland estates in order to improve or increase the native stocks. Red grouse at this time could readily be purchased from English dealers or sporting agents and sent north by rail for the princely sum of 30/- (£1.50) per brace, each brace consisting of one cock bird and two hens. The red grouse, that quintessential of all Highland game birds is actually of part-English ancestry.

RED DEER

The red deer, that most noble of all beasts of the chase, did not escape the attentions of the nineteenth century Highland game 'improvers'. In their quest for the perfect stag, capable of producing 'designer' heads or trophies, many lairds improved the herds in their deer forests by importing stags and hinds from English parks such as Welbeck, Windsor and Warnham, from

Exmoor, and from as far afield as Germany, Hungary and Ireland. According to the Warnham Park account books for 1898, a yearling stag could be purchased for £8 at this time while a three-year-old stag cost £10.

Trophy head of a Royal stag grassed at Ardvourlie, Isle of Harris 1865: courtesy of Sir Anthony Milbank, Bt. Red deer stags from English deer parks and elsewhere were regularly put down in Highland deer forests in order to improve the quality of the heads

Last but not least, a small coterie of sportsmen of independent means, both from London and the provinces, were also key players on the 'Highland Circuit'. Charles Caldwell Dallas, for instance, a wealthy New Forest bachelor, whose life was entirely devoted to fox hunting, yachting, skiing, pheasant shooting and big game hunting in Africa, took Highland shootings annually from the early 1880s until the late 1920s. He rented mainly mixed shootings on Hebridean islands, including Galson and Gress on Lewis, and Dunvegan on the Isle of Skye. Another hunting man, Alfred Brocklehurst from Melton Mowbray, a member of the Brocklehurst silk and banking dynasty, had a penchant for deer forests, taking Dundonnell, Dunbeath, Armadale, Glasletcailleach and various other forests, before securing a short lease over the 14,700 Rhifail Deer Forest in Sutherland from the Duke of Sutherland in 1898. The rental was £300/13/0 per annum (£17,155 in today's prices), together with a salmon beat for two rods on the river Naver for an additional £85 (or £4,850 today).

Charles Caldwell Dallas (left), a wealthy New Forest Sportsman who rented Highland shootings annually from the early 1880s until the late 1920s

Sadly, the outbreak of World War One in 1914 sounded the death knell of the 'Highland Circuit'. Punitive taxes imposed by the Lloyd George Government in the wake of the war not only affected the wealthy sportsmen who did the 'Circuit' each year but also prevented many of the estate owners from revitalising their by now run-down properties. Today, these sportsmen, who were rarely famous in any way and usually as anonymous as 'Lloyd's names', have virtually been 'air brushed' out of Highland folk history, remembered only by a golf or a football cup that they presented to a local club, a commemorative clock donated to a village hall, or a mouldering trophy stag's head hanging in an elderly crofter's cottage. Occasionally they left behind an inscribed antique silver christening mug given to the child of a ghillie or a gamekeeper who had been named in their honour, such as Charles Basil Fry MacDonald, Joseph Platt MacLennan and Edward Simon Marcus MacIver.

SHOOTING IN
EUROPE

BRITISH SPORTSMEN first began to travel to Europe in pursuit of partridges, pheasants, wild boar and other game during the late eighteenth century. They shot as invited guests on estates belonging to minor royalty and noblemen in countries such as Germany, Hungary, Bohemia and Austria. Their Victorian successors ventured further, journeying to Russia to shoot European bison, bears, wolves and capercailzie, or to Scandinavia in order to kill elk, ryper and willow grouse. Indeed, from the mid-Victorian period until outbreak of World War One in 1914, the Scandinavian countries of Norway, Denmark and Sweden

German deer shooting party c. 1910

were a popular destination for wealthy British shots and anglers. They either rented a sporting property on a seasonal basis for their exclusive use or stayed in a hotel with shootings and fishings attached.

European sporting tourism ceased for the duration of World War One. Sporting properties in many parts of the continent suffered from over-shooting or heavy poaching for food procurement purposes during the course of conflict and, in some cases, were ruined by the effects of deforestation or military activities. Thereafter, from the cessation of hostilities in 1919 until the declaration of World War Two in 1939, sportsmen tended to visit Europe (other than the Soviet Union) privately, shooting as guests of friends or on their own properties, rather than as paying Guns.

Game shooting for sporting purposes in Europe was discontinued once again during World War Two from 1939 until 1945 – although contemporary reports suggest that a number of British servicemen based on the Continent did manage to enjoy the occasional 'pot' at a bird, rabbit or deer in order to add variety to the normal fare on offer in the officers' mess. One former prisoner of war, who worked on a sugar beet farm in northern Germany during his captivity, reported that he was regularly sent out under supervision to shoot deer for the table, both for the benefit of the elderly guards and his fellow inmates. Sportsmen, however, began to return to Europe during the 1950s and early 1960s, attracted by chamois stalking on the Tyrol, roe stalking in Hungary and partridge shooting in Spain. Since this time Europe has become an increasingly popular destination for British shooting enthusiasts, many of whom make an annual pilgrimage to Spain in pursuit of partridges or travel to Hungary, Russia, Bulgaria, Poland, the Czech Republic and other former Eastern Bloc countries in order to shoot boar, wolves, bears and various species of deer.

The Tyrol

Situated in the Eastern Alps, the Tyrol region, which currently straddles the Austrian–Italian border, has attracted chamois shooting enthusiasts since the late nineteenth century. Prior to the outbreak of World War One in 1914, some British sportsmen actually owned or leased Tyrolean sporting estates, visiting annually

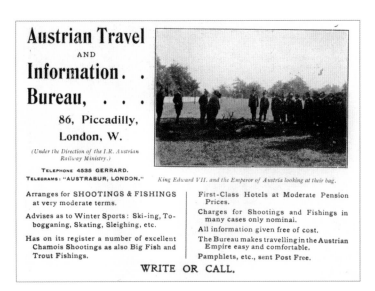

Advertisement for the Austrian Travel and Information Bureau 1905. The Bureau was able to arrange shooting packages for British sporting clients in the Tyrol and other parts of the Austrian Empire

during the autumn months in order to stalk chamois or to participate in specially organised chamois drives.

Sport at Gerlos

Captain Walter Waring of Lennel House in Berwickshire, a young army officer and a keen deer stalker, acquired the 70,000 acre Gerlos estate in the Tyrol in 1896 specifically for chamois shooting. Situated in a side valley of the Zillertal, the property was then in an extremely run-down condition due to over-poaching by the local peasantry, with the result that he and his guests only managed to secure a bag of three chamois during the course of his first season. Undaunted, the Captain managed to build up the chamois stocks over the next few years with the cooperation of his peasant neighbours, sharing out the chamois carcases amongst them at the end of each shoot, thus curtailing poaching activities. Thanks to judicious management, the annual chamois bag taken at Gerlos gradually increased from 3 in 1896 to 20 in 1899 and to 60 in 1903, eventually peaking at 155 beasts in 1910, a record year for the estate.

Sir Norman Lamont, Bt., the Scottish Liberal politician, who was a shooting guest at Gerlos in October 1910 when most of the chamois were killed, sent this report to a relative:

> 'We left Gerlos yesterday having killed 136 chamois in 14 days' shooting. There are far more now than ever – but the does have increased out of all proportion to the bucks. Walter shot very well, and got 35 to his own rifle. Self = 21. Bag as follows: October 10th, 4; 11th, 6; 12th, 12; 13th, 7; 14th, 7; 15th, 4; 17th, 14; 18th, 7; 19th, 15; 20th, 15; 21st, 10; 24th, 15; 25th, 6; 26th, 14. The weather has been very good, and we only had one day on which we could not go out.'

Sport at Gerlos was not for the faint hearted, though. According to surviving game books, chamois stalking invariably involved spending ten or twelve hours out in the field in pursuit of the quarry each day, walking over rough mountainous terrain at high altitudes (ranging from 1,250 to 3,208 metres above sea level), often in wintry conditions, in the company of a local 'jaeger' (professional hunter). If a drive had been arranged, Captain Waring and his guests would conceal themselves at various strategic points or 'stands' in the hills and fire at herds of chamois as they were driven towards them by a large team of beaters. Big bags were often taken in this way.

Chamois shooting party at Gerlos, 1903: courtesy of Sir Andrew de la Rue, Bt. Left to right: Sir Norman Lamont, Bt., Mark Fraser, George Milner, Captain Walter Waring

Entertaining local dignitaries

Guests at Gerlos during the Edwardian era included Captain Waring's friends and relatives together with prominent local people who were invited to a special end of season shoot and party. On 22 October 1901, for instance, according to an entry in the game book:

> 'Twenty two farmers and dignitaries appeared and two drives were held for roe in the woods, the drivers on this occasion being terriers. At the end of the day the bag consisted of 1 chamois, 4 roebucks, 3 does. A cask of beer and roasted doe followed at the inn, when the Herr Lieutenant's health was drunk, followed by those of Sir Clement Hill and the jaegers. A dance concluded the evening to the strains of the Gerlos Band, some thirty strong, lasting 'till 2 am.'

Gerlos was mothballed for the duration of World War One, although a couple of elderly gamekeepers were retained in order to keep poachers at bay and, apparently, were paid via a Swiss intermediary. Incredibly, the estate was in relatively good shape when Captain Waring returned at the end or the war, enabling him to continue chamois stalking on a more or less annual basis until his death in Munich in 1930, after which the property was sold.

Hungary

Since the late eighteenth century, British sportsmen have visited the central European country of Hungary in order to shoot game birds, deer and ground game on a sporadic basis in peacetime, whenever political conditions have been conducive. In times past, wealthy shots often participated in the vast *battues* which were regularly held on princely and noble estates where large bags of pheasants, partridges and hares were the order of the day. For example, the 2nd Earl of Malmesbury, who was a guest at one such *battue*, held by Prince Esterhazy at Hinkenbrunn on 17 October 1799, records that a total of eighteen sportsmen were out on the field, each having at least six guns and three loaders as well as a peasant to carry the guns. Between them they accounted for a bag of 788 pheasants, 6 partridges, 3 woodcock and 211 hares within the space of four hours.

Hungary gradually increased in popularity as a sporting destination during the nineteenth century and by the 1880s had become the 'partridge capital of Europe', annually attracting the elite of British and European shooting society who vied with each other to solicit invitations to partridge shoots on estates belonging to friends and acquaintances. Shoots on these properties were grandiose affairs with daily bags of between 1,000 and 2,000 birds (sometimes more) being killed. Guns were accommodated in castles or mansions, were given a substantial shoot lunch – eaten to the accompaniment of music played by a local band. According to some contemporary sources, if the Guns were unaccompanied by their wives or were single men, they would be provided with a female peasant girl to share their bed at night.

The St. Johann partridge shoot

The most prestigious partridge shoot at this time was undoubtedly St. Johann, situated on the Hungarian Marches, which comprised seventeen beats ranging from 8,000 to 10,000 acres in size, each of which was capable of yielding a daily bag of between 1,000 to 2,000 birds. It was owned by the railway financier, Baron Maurice de Hirsch who also leased the Wretham Hall partridge shoot in Norfolk and the state game preserves at Versailles in France. The property attracted a number of Britain's top shots during the late 1880s and early 1890s including the 2nd Marquess of Ripon, Lord Ashburton, Sir Harry Stonor and the Duke of Portland, as well as Edward, Prince of Wales who visited in 1890 and was a member of a team of Guns who bagged 11,000 partridges in a five-day period.

Lady Randolph Churchill, a regular social guest of Baron Hirsch, provided a brief glimpse of the daily routine at St. Johann during the partridge shooting season:

Lady Randolph Churchill

'Life at St. Johann was simple and healthy. After breakfast a fleet of Victorias paraded to drive those so inclined to the scene of slaughter, the postillions in hussar-like blue jackets, Hessian boots and shiny high-crowned hats. The battue then began. Six hundred beaters set off in a circle of some seven miles in circumference, directed by a head keeper sounding his bugle from a high tower. The Guns, rarely more than ten, were spread over a three-acre site in butts, walled in for their neighbours' safety, with fir branches.'

Sadly, to the dismay of his British shooting friends, Baron Hirsch sold St. Johann in 1895 to the German Chancellor, Prince Hohenloe for the sum of £300,000, principally because of his reluctance to pay the annual indemnity of £4,000 to his peasant neighbours for the damage his deer caused to their crops. However, many of these men continued to visit Hungary until the outbreak of World War One in order to take advantage of the superlative partridge shooting that was available on large estates in various parts of the country.

Hungary continued to offer some of the finest driven partridge shooting in Europe during the inter-war years, although apparently few British sportsmen visited the country during this period. Business was brisk, though, for Hungarian game dealers, who annually supplied hundreds of thousands of common or grey partridges and partridge eggs to shoots throughout Great Britain right up until the outbreak of World War Two in 1939, when the trade was suspended.

Changes in land management
Changes in land management and farming methods which took place in the aftermath of the war, when Hungary became a communist state, led to a dramatic decline in partridges stocks throughout the country, with the result that partridge shooting was generally disbanded. Thereafter, roe deer stalking became a popular sporting activity amongst the local elite, along with driven pheasant shooting (the pheasants were reared intensively on game farms and released amongst arable crops). From the early 1960s onwards, however, the Hungarian Government began to allow the various hunters' associations, which leased shooting rights from the state, to sell roe stalking and pheasant shooting facilities to parties of overseas sportsmen, primarily as a means of obtaining foreign currency.

Sporting tourism has gone from strength to strength since 1989, when

THE GERMAN MODE OF SHOOTING

The Reverend Dr Thomas Durnford, a Hampshire clergyman, experienced the German mode of shooting while on a visit to Westphalia in the 1770s but, nevertheless, considered that such a method of 'killing large quantities of game was by no means pleasing to an English sportsman'. He records:

'There are an infinite number of roads cut in the forests and woods to make the passage easy, and in them are many corn fields and open plains: in these open places are many little circular enclosures of wood full of bushes and thickets: the place for shooting is appointed by the Prince or Seigneur the day before; and the chasseurs of whom they have a vast number, and dogs are out early in the morning to the place appointed, and collect as many servants as they can both men, women, and children to each of whom is paid a small sum per day: these are all under the direction of the head chasseur who rides on horseback and gives his orders about the mode of marching, which is always done with great regularity in a line, all the chasseurs at proper distances forming themselves as Corporals in a Regiment: the chasseurs are all furnished with tambourines which are a small kind of drum, and each peasant holds in his hands a square piece of board and a kind of drumstick with which he makes a noise to rouse the game. The Prince or Seigneur goes in great style in a carriage with a multitude of servants on horseback: his friends or foreigners go in separate coaches: as soon as they arrive at the place appointed, and have taken their proper stations, the head chasseur gives orders to all the other chasseurs and peasants to begin their march regularly, and at equal distances from each other, the dogs marching with them, and in this manner drive the game before them, till they arrive within a little distance of the company, when they form the segment of a circle and in this manner drive the game out into one of the thickets or little woods, and in that form they all rush in regularly and drive out the game within reach of the Prince's or Seigneur's musket, and opposite to where he and his company have taken post, and then the firing begins. Each person is provided with a double barrelled gun, and a multitude of servants stand behind the Seigneur and his company, and are continually employed in charging and delivering fresh guns, so that an uninterrupted firing is kept up as long as the game continues flying or running out of the woods.'

Shooting in snowy conditions in Hungary: courtesy of Pete Jagger

Hungary dispensed with communism and became a parliamentary state. The country now attracts a large number of British sportsmen every year who come in pursuit of exceptional driven pheasant and duck shooting; red, roe, or fallow deer stalking; or mouflon and boar hunting. Perhaps, unsurprisingly, given the quality and variety of game available, a number of British gamekeepers have chosen to relocate to Hungary in recent years in order to improve shoots and to enhance their curricula vitae.

Norway

A popular destination for wealthy anglers from the mid-Victorian period until the outbreak of World War One in 1914, Norway was also something of a mecca for game shots who were prepared to traverse rough terrain in pursuit of elk, deer, black game, ryper and capercailzie. Quite a number of British sportsmen owned or leased property in Norway at this time along with associated riparian and shooting rights. Some also rented 'elk rights' from neighbouring farmers which allowed them to kill a stated number of elk upon payment of a fee of between £5 and £15, provided that they had obtained an elk shooting licence from the Norwegian authorities.

Deer shooting on the island of Hitra

Sir Francis Denys, Bt., a member of the British Diplomatic Service, visited Norway on a number of occasions during the 1890s and the early 1900s in order to shoot and fish. He spent six weeks on the Norwegian island of Hitra (situated some 130 kilometres south-west of Trondheim) in 1899 in pursuit of red deer and other game. He went as a 'paying Gun' in a party organised by the explorer, big game hunter and Conservative Member of Parliament for St. Helens, Henry Seton-Karr, who rented the sporting rights over a portion of the island. Accompanied by Mr Seton-Karr, Mr and Mrs Armitage and a Mr Congreve, Sir Francis left Hull aboard the *SS Tasso* at 5 p.m. on 10 August 1899 and reached Hitra on Sunday 13 August at 8 p.m., having changed ships at Kristiansund. Extracts taken from his 'sporting journal', filled in on a daily basis throughout his stay on the island of Hitra, provide us with some brief vignettes of his shooting and stalking activities:

'16 AUGUST 1899

Two deer drives on Langvard and Heonedaal, short drives with 6 beaters out. On the first drive a small stag stood for five minutes within 7 yards and never saw me, and a three year old stag and a hind galloped past me. As venison was wanted, I fired through thick timber at the stag and missed. On the second drive Seton-Karr secured a 17 stone stag with velvet on, and Mr Armitage said he wounded another. Four hinds passed me only.

23 AUGUST 1899

Out on Storfield after 4 pm. Had an easy stalk at 7 pm in the open on top of the field. Just as I was making ready to shoot, Daniel Strom, who was with me, gave an unearthly yell which frightened me as much as it did the stag. I took a hurried aim, and fortunately the stag dropped, shot through the neck at 80 yards. He was in velvet with a hideous head of no points. He weighed 17 stone, 2lbs. clean. Saw one other stag and six hinds.

5 SEPTEMBER 1899

Left the house at 5 am. Had the luck to spy a really big stag feeding on the flat directly to the left of Elsfield Pass. A successful stalk by Brettle in a very light shifty breeze got me within 110 yards, and I shot him across the little valley at 6.40 am.

Returned home at 7.15 am. Deer drive after breakfast, 5 or 6 hinds seen. Went out with our guns after lunch. Self: 3 black game. Mr Armitage: 2 ryper. Congreve: a baby stag.

26 SEPTEMBER 1899
Three deer drives took place, at the Flats, North Elsfield and South Elsfield. On the drive at North Elsfield, at dusk, a good stag came slowly to my stand and I dropped

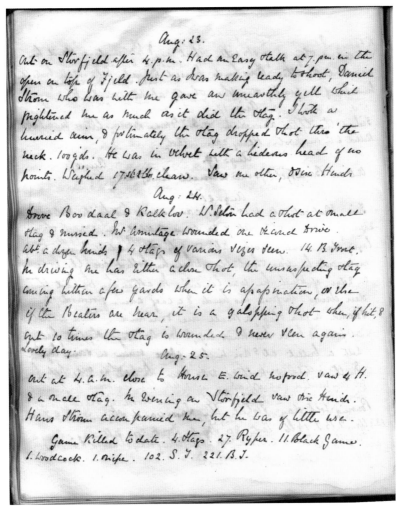

A page of Sir Francis Denys' journal from 1899

him. An easy shot, he weighed 250 lbs. and was a switch. The beaters alleged that they moved 15 stags, but I only saw the one that I killed; the other rifles saw none. This is supposed to be the best ground for stags on the island! Some 8 or 10 hinds were seen.

2 OCTOBER 1899

Shot 4 black game, 2 ryper and 1 snipe between 10 am and 1.30. We then took the boat from Balness to Langvard. Saw what we fancied were two stags, but we could not stalk them as they went in the wrong direction. A fine old capercailzie rose at my feet and settled in a tree. I shot him with the rifle at 80 yards and took his carcase to Trondheim to be stuffed. He weighed 11 lbs. Home 8 pm. Very fine day.'

In all, Sir Francis Denys shot or stalked on a total of thirty-eight days during his sporting sojourn on the island of Hitra, ending his visit on 3 October 1899, when he killed a four-year-old stag specifically 'to take the haunches back to England'. He left Norway on 4 October and returned to England 'overland via Copenhagen'. Sir Francis and his party killed a total of 20 stags (of which 6 were heavy stags), 35 ryper, 52 black game, 410 brown trout, 146 sea trout. He personally accounted for a bag of 8 stags, 30 black game, 5 ryper and 1 capercailzie.

SHOOTING IN THE VICINITY OF FLORENCE

'There is good woodcock shooting in the Appenines; but as the ground is all private property, a sportsman must, in addition to the porta de'arma and shooting certificate or licence from the government, have the permission of some proprietor. In the Maremma there is capital woodcock and wildfowl shooting, roe deer and wild boar; but unless he knows some of the large landed gentry of the country this will be out of his reach. In February there are plenty of wildfowl about Lago Bientina, which is free; and during the winter, or from November to March, there are plenty of snipe and waterfowl in the marshes that surround the lake, which is between Leghorn and Florence, but, as the marsh is very dangerous, it should not be tried without a guide.'

The Field 23 October 1858

Russia

Prior to the outbreak of the Russian Revolution in 1917, most of the major Russian towns and cities supported a small community of British businessmen who were engaged in trading activities of one kind or another. Many of these men were sporting enthusiasts and belonged to the shooting clubs that had been set up by the Tsarist Government at the commencement of the twentieth century in order to control hunting and to conserve game stocks. Capercailzie shooting, bear stalking and wolf driving all appear to have been popular pastimes amongst expatriate sportsmen at this time.

Organising a wolf drive

Organising a wolf drive was 'something of a scientific affair', according to an un-named British businessman who belonged to a St. Petersburg shooting club during the early 1900s:

> 'The club employed a professional tracker or *psquichi* who relied upon the information from villagers when a wolf pack was in their neighbourhood. He would follow their tracks (easily discernible in the snow) and when they commenced to circle this was an infallible sign that they were going to 'lay up' in a wood. He then dumped the carcase of a horse or cow as near to the pack as possible and then ringed the whole area with 'flags'. Flags 'were stout whipcord at least a mile in length,

Members of a Russian shooting club c. 1905

supported on stakes and carrying coloured bunting at short intervals. The wolves will not violate the flags so our *psquichi* summons his employers, makes gaps in the flags and places a Gun covering each gap. Local villagers impressed as beaters by the lure of scarce roubles then drive the animals towards the Guns. For this sport the Russian aristocrat normally used a 12-bore gun with a charge of slugs, but one expatriate Englishman was convinced that a 'paradox' rifled shotgun with No.5 shot in one barrel and a bullet in t'other was the best tool for the job.'

British owned sporting estates

Surprisingly, given the volatile political situation in Russia during the early years of the twentieth century, a number of wealthy British businessmen acquired large Russian sporting properties. Mr L. Morton, for instance, purchased the Byatch estate near Sednev in the Ukraine around 1903 specifically in order to have a driven pheasant shoot (the Tsar, apparently, had an English style pheasant shoot on his game preserves near St. Petersburg) and imported two English gamekeepers to set up and run the shoot with the help of local keepers. This enterprise, however, was short lived and was disbanded after peasants stormed the estate and burned down the mansion in the October Revolution of 1905.

Some of the more adventurous British big game hunters took advantage of the sport available in Russia, too, during the late Victorian and the Edwardian periods, organising expeditions to remote areas in order to shoot bears, European bison, elk and other quadrupeds. The noted hunter and explorer St. George Littledale, and the well-known shot the 6th Duke of Portland, were amongst the many sporting tourists who visited parts of the Russian empire to shoot and fish during the final decades of Tsarist rule, after which sporting estates came under communist control and were broken up and unrestricted travel throughout the country became a thing of the past.

Monte Carlo

Universally known for its world famous casino, the tiny Mediterranean state of Monte Carlo attracted wealthy British gamblers outside the shooting season from the early 1870s until the outbreak of World War Two. In addition, many of the nation's top shots came to shoot at live pigeons fired from traps at a special shooting range situated in the grounds of the Gun Club. During the Edwardian era, the 2nd Marquess of Ripon, Prince Victor Duleep Singh, and other shooting legends visited annually in order to compete against their European counterparts in the 'pigeon' Grand Prix du Casino. The tournament offered £250 in prize money and a handsome silver trophy. The Grand Prix de Cloture marked the end of the Monte Carlo pigeon shooting season. Some of the more enthusiastic pigeon shots also participated in Le Championnat Triennal, which was held at the Gun Club every three years. Live pigeon shooting from traps (banned in Great Britain in 1921) continued to take place in Monte Carlo until 1960 when pigeons were replaced by 'robot pigeons', although by this time the sport had become less fashionable amongst British and Continental sporting tourists. The Monte Carlo pigeon shooting range survived until 1972, when it was demolished due to lack of use.

Lord Illingworth, a Yorkshire landowner, competing in a pigeon shooting tournament at the Gun Club at Monte Carlo c. 1935

Shooting driven partridges at Brea de Tajo, Spain: courtesy of Roxtons

Spain

Spain has become an increasingly popular destination for British sporting tourists over the past fifty years or so, annually attracting a large number of discerning Guns who come specifically for the superlative driven red-legged partridge shooting on offer in many areas. Sportsmen both young and old find Spanish partridge shooting an exhilarating experience and not only relish the opportunity to participate in shoots with an expected daily bag of between 400 and 700 or more birds, but also enjoy the good food and fine wines that are available.

Sporting lets were pioneered in the 1960s by the Landaluce family, who founded Cacerias Azor, a dedicated Spanish partridge shooting agency that currently provides shooting facilities for overseas clients over a 25,000 hectare estate in the La Mancha region. Shooting in Spain can either be obtained directly from local shoot managers such as Cacerias Azor, or from many of the leading British sporting agencies which can offer tailor made packages including accommodation, meals and flights plus the loan of shotguns if necessary.

Perhaps, unsurprisingly, given the attractions of red-legged partridge shooting in Spain, a number of leading British shots have purchased or leased Spanish sporting properties at one time and another over the past half-century. The late Sir Joseph Nickerson, for example, a well-known shooting enthusiast and crack-shot, acquired the Nombela estate near Escalona in the 1980s which he operated along English lines until his death in 1990. While the Duke of Westminster, another notable shot, took a ten-year lease on the La Garganta estate in Castilla La Mancha in 2002, a prestigious shoot owned by Prince Franz, Duke of Bavaria, which boasts partridges, red deer, roe deer and wild boar.

On a historical note, King Alfonso XIII was one of the first sportsmen to practise driven partridge shooting in Spain. Impressed by the sport that he had experienced as a guest on the royal estate at Windsor during the early years of the twentieth century, he established a driven partridge shoot on his private estate at Casa de Campo. He imported a consignment of red-legged partridges from Britain and hired an English gamekeeper, Mr Watts, in order to get things up and running in the correct way.

Ireland

Geographically an integral part of the British Isles, with Northern Ireland remaining under British rule and the Republic of Ireland forming an independent EU member state, Ireland has been renowned for its exceptional woodcock and snipe shooting since the late eighteenth century. It has attracted generations of sportsmen to its shores in pursuit of these game birds. In addition, the country offers good walked-up grouse shooting in some areas, superlative wildfowling, challenging rough shooting and English-style driven pheasant shooting on some of the larger sporting estates, particularly those in the north.

Shooting party at Mount Juliet, Co. Kilkenny c. 1900

Game shooting, however, was something of a low key activity amongst the Anglo-Irish Ascendancy landowners during the late eighteenth and the first half of the nineteenth centuries, the great majority of whom were avid fox hunting enthusiasts rather than shooters. Their estates were managed principally for hunting, although many boasted a large deer park either to provide beasts for the chase or venison for the table.

The landed gentry of the day invariably preserved game as a matter of course but were more than happy for English friends, relatives and acquaintances to shoot over their properties on a 'grace and favour' basis. They gladly provided accommodation for them. As Richard Thornhill wrote in 1804:

> 'If a sportsman is fond of woodcock shooting, it will pay him well for his trouble to take a trip to Ireland… As to asking leave, it is needless; as the only cause of jealousy that can subsist between the visitor and the owner of the ground will be for not acquainting him of his coming, in order that he might have it in his power to receive him in the usual hospitable manner, by providing beaters to show him sport, giving him the best of fare, a bottle of good claret, a sincere and hearty welcome, assuring his guest the longer he stays and honours him with his company, the more welcome he is, and the happier he will make him.'

Sporting lets

Conscious of the income that could be derived from charging English sportsmen for the privilege of shooting woodcock, snipe and other game birds, some of the more impoverished Irish landowners started to let out the sporting rights over their properties during the early nineteenth century and built lodges to accommodate their tenants. Sporting lets of this kind, particularly if they included salmon and sea trout fishing in rivers and lochs, and wildfowling, found a ready market both amongst wealthy woodcock shooting enthusiasts and anglers and many of the more impecunious sportsmen who could not afford to rent a Scottish sporting property for the season. Indeed, by the early 1900s, according to Lord Granville Gordon, parts of Ireland had become: 'the standby of half-pay officers and others with slender incomes, who make great account of its snipe and other rough shooting merely because they can afford nothing better.'

Shooting was generally eschewed by members of the landed Anglo-Irish Ascendancy in favour of hunting until the late Victorian period when proprietors of large estates began to establish driven pheasant, partridge and grouse shoots in order to entertain their English and Scottish social peers. Many recruited an English or a Scottish head gamekeeper and a team of local under-keepers to preserve game on their properties, and imported vast quantities of pheasant and partridge eggs for hatching and rearing under broody hens or consignments of mature birds in order to stock their woods and coverts. Further, in 1891, a group of prominent Irish landowners founded the Irish Game Protection Association to look after the interests of the shooting fraternity, employing a resident inspector in any county where subscriptions exceeded £50 per annum.

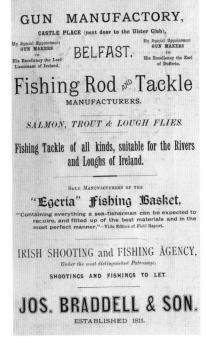

*Advertisement for
Joseph Braddell & Son
of Belfast, gunmakers and
sporting agents 1892*

Big bags on top Irish shoots

Some of the top Irish shoots quickly gained a reputation for comparatively large bags of pheasants, woodcock and other game at this time and began to attract well-known British sportsmen, including several members of the royal family. The Prince of Wales (later King George V), for example, spent several days woodcock shooting at Ashford in Co. Galway in January 1905, while HRH the Duke of Connaught (a brother of King Edward VII) visited various shoots in Ireland as an invited guest in the early 1900s, in particular Glaslough in Co. Monaghan, home of the Leslie family, and Tandergee Castle in Co. Armagh, Irish seat of the 9th Duke of Manchester, where he felt impelled to comment to his host about the large number of 'rudderless' cock pheasants that were running around. These pheasants had been specially sent over from England in wicker hampers for the shoot but had had their tail feathers removed for ease of transit.

The gamekeeping staff at Baronscourt, Co. Tyrone c. 1900:
courtesy of Abercorn Estates/ www.barons-court.com

A number of impressive bags were taken on Irish sporting properties during the late nineteenth and the early twentieth centuries. Sir Victor Brooke shot a total of 740 rabbits in one day in his park at Colebrooke in Co. Fermanagh in 1885; 338 grouse were killed by a party of thirteen Guns on the Sheepshanks beat at Powerscourt in Co. Wicklow on 25 September 1890; 967 pheasants were shot by a team of nine Guns at Moyne House in Queen's Co. on 10 November 1909; 228 woodcock were brought down by six Guns on Lord Ardilaun's estate at Ashford in Co. Galway (considered to be the best woodcock shoot in the world) on 31 January 1910 – an all-time record for a day's woodcock shooting in Great Britain. Last but not least, a grand total of 467 wood pigeon were bagged by Mr Cecil Fitzherbert on the Abbeyleix estate in Queen's Co. on 1 December 1911.

Shoots throughout Ireland were scaled down drastically following the outbreak of World War One in 1914, when sportsmen and gamekeepers joined the armed services in order to fight for Great Britain. Sporting properties were either lightly kepered or abandoned for the duration, with the result that game stocks became depleted in many districts due to a combination of over-poaching and an increase in the avian vermin population.

SHOOTING REPORT

Nine days' shooting at Shelton Abbey, Co. Wicklow from November 11th to January 15th resulted in a total bag of 3,571 pheasants, 24 woodcock, 9 snipe, 1 wild duck, 3 hares, and 4 rabbits. The following are the numbers of pheasants shot each day: 676, 1,008, 513, 737, 56, 167, 229, 65, and 120.

W.J. Spearing, head gamekeeper to the
Earl of Wicklow
The Gamekeeper February 1914

The Troubles

The Troubles that took place in the aftermath of the war in 1919 and 1920 made it difficult for Irish landowners to rebuild their shoots or to invite English guests over for rough shooting and fishing. Gamekeepers were obliged to combine game preservation with security duties in order to try and protect castles and mansions from entry by the IRA. Large numbers of sporting guns and rifles were taken by the IRA in raids on country house gun rooms or were confiscated by the police for various reasons. Game shooting permits were withdrawn in certain districts, if considered necessary by the authorities.

Nearly two hundred country houses were destroyed in the Civil War which took place in the wake of the declaration of the Irish Free State in 1921, with the result that shooting and game preservation ceased on the surrounding estates. This was to signal the end of many large sporting estates in the south of Ireland. The high demesne wall which usually surrounded these properties, seen by many people as a symbol of oppression, was often reduced to waist or field fence height. In many instances, the land passed to the Land Commission and was divided up into small farms which were allocated to local people.

Shooting rights in the Republic of Ireland

The shooting rights over vast tracts of southern Ireland, now known as the Republic of Ireland, subsequently came into the possession of the Land Commission and were either vested with farming tenants, leased to hotels and guest houses or, in the case of some of the more valuable shootings, retained by the Commission which not only let them out to English and Irish sportsmen on a weekly, monthly or seasonal basis but issued an annual letting catalogue. Some of the wealthier Irish landowners who could afford to retain a large sporting estate and a gamekeeping team gradually revitalised organised walked-up and driven shoots during the late 1920s and the 1930s, although by the 1950s and '60s high labour costs had forced many to take in paying Guns to make ends meet.

Southern Ireland continues to offer some of the finest woodcock shooting and wildfowling available in the British Isles at the present time, despite the many changes that have taken place over the past century or so, both politically and in land management. The country is also a popular destination for those in search of mixed rough shooting, salmon and sea trout fishing and wild brown trout angling, or combined shooting and fishing packages. Driven shoots are now few and far between, although some exceptional driven pheasant and duck shooting can be found on a small number of estates in Co. Wicklow. It goes without saying that the great majority of Irish shoots are now run along commercial lines, either by private landowners and syndicates or by hoteliers.

Game shooting in Northern Ireland

Game shooting in the six Ulster counties which chose to remain under British

High birds at Baronscourt, Co. Tyrone: courtesy of Abercorn Estates/ www.barons-court.com

Rule after 1921 was largely unaffected, although many landowners were eventually forced to take in paying Guns or set up commercial shoots in order to defray shoot operating costs. In fact, a number of the great shoots in Ulster, such as Baronscourt in Co. Tyrone, Ballywalter Park in Co. Down (where the Duke of York – later King George VI – shot in 1924) and Colebrooke Park in Co. Fermanagh, are still held in very high regard in British and overseas shooting circles.

RABBIT SHOOTING WITH CRABS

In the coastal areas of Co. Galway in the west of Ireland a very novel method of rabbit shooting was formerly practised by the local men. They took live crabs from the sea, then secured a lighted candle onto their backs before putting them into warrens to flush out rabbits to the waiting Guns.

SHOOTING
WORLDWIDE

OVER THE PAST THREE CENTURIES OR SO, British men have travelled to all corners of the globe as colonists, soldiers, diplomats, explorers, businessmen or simply as tourists. In the days of the British Empire, expatriates invariably arrived at their destinations accompanied by a rod and a gun, especially if they were on a tour of duty lasting for several years. They eagerly sought out whatever sporting opportunities might happen to be available within reach of their new homes.

Safari hunter with a 'trophy' buffalo in Tanzania: courtesy of Coenraad Vermaak Safaris

Sportsmen of independent means began to visit Africa and India during the first half of the nineteenth century in pursuit of elephants, lions, tigers and other kinds of big game. They undertook expeditions to the interiors, in search of the best hunting grounds for particular species, shooting 'trophies of the chase' and collecting specimens for European museums. Some also travelled to North America at this time in order to shoot bison, bears, caribou, moose, wild turkey and other indigenous species of game.

Big game hunting in Africa, particularly in South and East Africa, and in India became a popular pastime amongst the aristocracy and the landed gentry during the late Victorian and the Edwardian periods. Some went on

Lion hunters in West Africa 1936

safari expeditions on an almost annual basis, leaving Britain in February after the pheasant shooting season had ended and returning in late spring or early summer in time for the start of the Scottish fishing and deer stalking season. Sporting tourism to Africa and the Indian subcontinent ceased during World War One but enjoyed a resurgence during the 1920s, particularly in Kenya and Tanganyika, where many wealthy Britons settled and acquired large plantation estates which abounded with game. India became an increasingly less attractive destination for British sportsmen following independence in 1947, after which many quarry species were decimated by poachers and farmers. South Africa, Zambia, Uganda and Tanzania (formerly known as Tanganyika), however, continue to attract large numbers of British sporting enthusiasts at the present time, although most now participate in shorter safaris due to cost and time constraints.

Today, British sportsmen also go to South America to shoot wild duck and to the USA to shoot quail, chukar partridges, pheasants, wild turkey, deer and other quarry species.

India

Big game shooting, commonly known as *shikar*, was introduced into India during the eighteenth century by British Army officers and civil servants employed by the Honourable East India Company. Often the younger sons of members of the aristocracy or landed gentry, these men went out in pursuit of tigers, bears, antelopes, elephants and other exotic quarry species during their leisure time, usually as guests of Indian maharajas or princes on their private game preserves. Over the years the term *shikar* began to embrace a number of other sporting activities brought to India by the British Raj or ruling class, including game bird shooting, angling, pig sticking and fox or jackal hunting carried out by fox hounds imported from England.

His Excellency Sir John Anderson, Governor of Bengal (right) duck shooting on the Seali Beel in West Bengal c. 1932

The Indian Empire

Following the formation of the Indian Empire in 1857, the British Government, who took over the administration of India and the various Indian armed services from the Honourable East India Company, began to set up vast game preserves in many parts of the subcontinent, often in states under the control of native rulers. These preserves, sometimes divided up into a number of dedicated shooting beats and equipped with luxurious lodges and bungalows, were then set aside for the use of native rulers and their guests, military personnel and visiting dignitaries from Great Britain and other parts of the empire.

Aware of the need to conserve Indian game species for the benefit of sportsmen, the British administration gradually introduced legislation controlling

Shooting party in India c. 1910

shooting seasons and bag restrictions in certain areas, culminating in the Indian Game Protection Act of 1912. In addition, virtually every state had its own subsidiary regulations requiring sportsmen to purchase shooting licences, protecting sacred birds such as the peacock. They also operated vermin bounty systems whereby any person who killed wild dogs, wolves, leopards and other predatory creatures could claim a cash payment upon production of the skins to the secretary of the local Game Preservation Department.

Shooting expeditions in the days of the Raj

Shooting expeditions in the days of the British Raj were often ostentatious affairs involving hundreds of native attendants and beaters who accompanied groups of VIP sportsmen deep into the jungle in pursuit of tigers, panthers, bears or rhinoceros. Large encampments were set up where Guns could sleep in luxurious mosquito-proof tents and dine in style on tinned provisions and wines imported from Fortnum & Mason in London. Guns often travelled from beat to beat upon horseback on these events and shot at their quarry from a *howdah* mounted on the back of an elephant.

The more impecunious sportsmen, such as junior army officers or middle-class civil servants, rarely took part in large scale big game hunts unless extremely well connected. Instead, they shot snipe on the numerous areas of

*Ghurka attendants posing with a panther killed by a British sportsman
at Mammad, India 1918*

bog found in many parts of India, rode out with the Madras, the Ootacmund, the Peshewar Vale or one of the other British-style hunts in pursuit of the fox or the jackal, or fished for Indian Trout, Mahseer or Tengara, all of which could be caught in rivers and streams throughout the Indian subcontinent.

Snipe shooting in Madras c. 1920

Some impressive bags of big game

Some impressive bags of game were taken by sportsmen in India during the period of the British Raj. For example, the Viceroy of India, Lord Irwin, and a party of Guns shooting at Sariska in 1929 accounted for a bag of 10,000 imperial sand grouse; in 1938, the Maharaja of Jaipur and a number of guests brought down a total of 4,273 wildfowl on a specially created area of wetland at Keoladeo Ghana; while on an unspecified date during the late Victorian period, Mr Lionel Inglis, a well-known sportsman, shot a leopard in Kashmir measuring 9 feet, 1 inch, believed to be an all-time record length for a leopard.

Inevitably, the enthusiasm for *shikar* in India during the nineteenth century led to the establishment of firms of specialist gunsmiths who manufactured or imported guns and rifles from Great Britain for expatriate sportsmen; tailors such as Hall & Anderson of Calcutta who produced khaki shooting outfits and *topees* which could be worn in extreme climatic conditions of heat or humidity; and camping equipment suppliers who provided mosquito-proof tents, portable washing equipment, folding card tables and other accessories necessary for comfortable sporting expeditions. A number of taxidermy businesses were set up in large towns enabling members of the Raj to have their 'trophies of the chase' stuffed and mounted. Eventually, these trophies would be sent back to Britain to be displayed and admired in country houses or suburban villas.

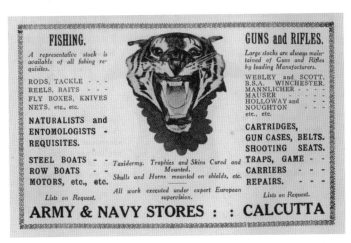

Advertisement for the Army & Navy Stores, Calcutta; one of the principal suppliers of sporting equipment and services to members of the Raj

Not surprisingly, a thriving sporting press flourished in India throughout the late nineteenth and early twentieth centuries, producing the *Indian Field* and various other periodicals devoted to the pursuit of *shikar*. Numerous books were published on the subject as well as several annual handbooks, including the *Hog Hunters Annual*, which ran from 1928 until 1939, and the *Indian Field Shikar Book*, an indispensable guide which gave in-depth information about every species of bird, beast or fish to be found on the subcontinent and contained lists of game regulations for each state.

The post-independence era

Shikar continued to be a popular pastime amongst members of the British armed forces and civil service based in India right up until the nation was granted independence in 1947. Thereafter, many species of big game suffered at the hands of farmers who wanted to protect their crops, and poachers who were out to profit from the sale of animal by-products such as elephant tusks. Sadly, today, despite the intervention of the World Wildlife Fund and other conservation organisations, stocks of tigers and various other animals formerly preserved and hunted by sportsmen are now perilously low.

INDIAN GAME BOOKS

Unlike standard game books, which contain a quarry species list on each page, books produced for the Indian market in the days of the Raj were divided into two sections: one for 'Small Game', with columns for game birds, ground game and fish; the other for 'Big Game' which consisted of bison, tiger, panther, deer and other large quadrupeds.

South America

Many British professional men travelled to South America during the late nineteenth and the early twentieth centuries in order to construct the railway network, to develop mineral mines, to manage large scale farming operations or as members of the Diplomatic Service. A surprising number took advantage of whatever sport was available locally, be it duck shooting, ostrich shooting or guanaco stalking. Those based in the Falkland Islands in the pre-sheep farming days even organised special wild cattle drives, the cattle being driven towards posted Guns by teams of local gaucho (cowboy) beaters!

Sir Francis Denys, Bt., for example, British Chargé D'Affaires in Mexico from 1887 to 1890, was invariably accompanied by rod and gun on his many fact finding missions around the country. He went shooting on a regular basis on *enstancias* belonging to wealthy Mexicans, taking a particular interest in duck and the

Sir Francis Denys, Bt., British Chargé D'Affaires in Mexico 1887–1890

rose-coloured spoon bill, which he considered to be a 'very sporting quarry species'. He records one memorable occasion in his game book in 1890 when he spent a day on horseback at the edge of a lake at Luavachena shooting at snipe, teal and duck, accounting for thirty-five head, all of which were retrieved by a 'naked Indian boy' who ran into the water after each bird had been shot.

Duck shooting at the Hacienda de Escalera

On 27 December 1887, while staying as a guest with Don Pablo de Escandon at the Hacienda de Escalera at Guadalupe, Sir Francis participated in a somewhat unusual, if barbaric, form of duck shooting on an area of wetland belonging to his host. His game book includes a brief account of the morning's proceedings:

'A large party of 10 Guns embarked in two enormous punts propelled by Indians with poles, and amused themselves in slaughtering the ducks crippled by the discharge of the Amarda. This instrument of destruction consists of a battery of old guns and gas-pipes fired simultaneously by an Indian at the duck, which are moved up by men towards it. On this occasion about 60 were killed, the sportsmen assassinating 26 other cripples. This sport not being very amusing I proposed to Escandon to go after snipe, but as he wanted to return to his guests we walked only once up and down the marsh. I shot 3 snipe and 3 duck. An immense Mexican lunch and "moule" completed the morning.'

Happily, duck shooting practices in Mexico have improved since Sir Francis' day. Indeed, over the past half century or so, Mexico has become one of the world's premier duck shooting destinations and boasts a number of exclusive country club-based shoots where sportsmen can stay in deluxe shooting lodge accommodation for a week or more at a time.

East Africa

Following the colonisation of East Africa by the British and the Germans during the late Victorian period, wealthy British sporting tourists began to visit Kenya, Uganda, British Somaliland and German East Africa (part of which was ceded to Britain after the end of World War One and became Tanganyika), attracted by the prospect of shooting large numbers of elephants, lions, giraffes, rhinoceros, zebras and other kinds of game, both big and small. The sportsmen of the day spent large sums of money planning and organising big game hunting expeditions, or safaris, into the interior of East Africa, hiring teams of ox-drawn wagons to transport their camping and sporting equipment and large numbers of natives to attend to their needs. For example, in 1913, the 5th Duke of Sutherland and the American millionaire and big game hunter, Paul Rainey, engaged nearly two hundred native porters, guides, skinners, gun bearers, cooks and boy assistants plus a pack of hounds in order to undertake a month-long lion shooting safari in Kenya. The duke also brought along a stalker from his Scottish estate to ensure that things ran smoothly.

World War One and beyond

Big game hunting safari expeditions in East Africa ceased during World War One due to Allied and German military activities in the region. Thereafter, under the terms of the Treaty of Versailles in 1919, the German East African colony was apportioned between Great Britain, Belgium and Portugal. Kenya, Uganda and Tanganyika became the principal big game hunting destinations in East Africa.

Lions could be shot free of charge in Kenya and Uganda...

... but shooting an elephant incurred a premium of £15:
both photographs courtesy of Marcus Janssen

Conscious of the need to conserve game stocks in these countries, the authorities introduced a licensing system for locals and overseas visitors which placed a bag limit on certain quarry species. In Kenya and Uganda a visitor's licence entitled the holder on payment of £100 to shoot 6 buffalo bulls, 6 oryx beiss, 6 Grevy's zebra, 8 topi, 20 Coke's hartebeest, 6 Hunter's antelope, 12 wildebeest, 10 reedbuck and 10 each of Peter's and Soemmering's gazelles. Lions were free and an unlimited number could be shot but a premium of £15 was payable for an elephant, £45 for two elephants, £15 for a giraffe, £5 for a rhinoceros and £15 for two rhinoceros. Similar restrictions applied in Tanganyika but British soldiers serving in Africa or India could purchase a concessionary licence for only £15. Separate licences were needed to shoot big game in each country. Going on a safari expedition was an expensive business.

Safari by motor car and lorry

Sportsmen began to utilise motorised transport to replace horse drawn wagons, pack mules and ponies for East African safari expeditions during the early 1920s, enabling them to cover greater distances and to shoot a large bag of game within a much shorter space of time than in the past. Commenting on the changes that had taken place in Tanganyika in a letter to *The Times* in the 1920s, Mr G.H. Anderson, an experienced big game hunter observed:

There plenty Big Gan Huntin and . . .

Sport of every kind in KENYA, UGANDA and TANGANYIKA

Nowhere else in the world can be found such abundance of big game—such a variety of wild li so many sporting attractions.

The Kenya and Uganda Railways and the Tangan Railways provide up-to-date and efficient rail and services to all parts of these magnificent Em Territories.

Full particulars and illustrated literature will be supplied free on request to the Railways Representative

(East African Office) GRAND BUILDINGS,
(Strand Entrance) **TRAFALGAR SQUARE, LONDON, W**

KENYA & UGANDA Railways & Harbour and the TANGANYIKA RAILWAY

Advertisement promoting rail travel for sportsmen in Kenya, Uganda and Tanganyika 1937

'Nearly all shooting parties enter this country from Kenya with motor lorries and probably a light touring car. And shooting parties go down there generally for about a five to six weeks shoot and come back with an average of five lions a Gun (they are now limited to five in Tanganyika), also buffalo, rhino, cheetah and probably a leopard or two and about eighteen other different species of game. They get a bag in a six weeks' shoot which in the old days with porters would take seven months or more shooting and working for it... I am sorry to say that a great deal of the game has actually been shot from cars. All this really makes a farce of the whole thing and to my mind very little sport. There is practically no hunting required and it only means that the so-called 'big game hunter' comes back at the end of six weeks with a fine bag obtained with practically no work, absolutely no hardships and very little danger.'

National parks and game reserves

In addition to implementing licensing as a conservation measure, a number of national parks and game reserves were established in East Africa during the inter-war years in order to provide sanctuaries for the declining big game populations and to protect elephants and other species from the predations of professional 'white hunters', who killed solely for commercial gain rather than for sporting purposes. Sadly, such sanctuaries did little to deter poachers who continued to take game whenever the opportunity arose.

Safari activities, however, were scaled down dramatically following the outbreak of World War Two in 1939, although game stocks were depleted in many parts of East Africa during the war years due to poaching for food procurement purposes. In the aftermath of the war, civil disturbances and political unrest in the region prevented motorised game safaris from continuing in many areas. This situation lasted until the mid-1960s, by which time Kenya, Uganda and Tanganyika (which became Tanzania in 1964) had all gained their independence from Great Britain and had become self-governing republics.

The safari situation today

Since the late 1960s, big game safaris in East Africa have becoming increasingly popular, and benefit the economies of the countries involved. Clients range from

Modern-day safari essentials: courtesy of Coenraad Vermaak safaris

On safari – twenty-first century style: courtesy of Marcus Janssen

sportsmen in pursuit of 'trophies of the chase', to wildlife enthusiasts and photographers who prefer to shoot with a camera rather than a rifle. Hunting was banned in Kenya in 1977 for conservation reasons, with the result that Uganda and Tanzania are now the main safari centres.

Shanghai

Situated in the Yangtze Delta in North China, the city and port of Shanghai was home to a large British community from the end of First Opium War in 1842 until the Japanese occupied the Shanghai International Settlement in 1941. Merchants, financiers, ship owners, administrators and others settled in the city in order to carry out trade between China and the rest of the world. Many of these men were avid sportsmen and took full advantage of the numerous game shooting opportunities that were available in the surrounding countryside where quarry species included snipe, pheasants, bamboo partridge, quail, woodcock, hill pigeon and a wide variety of wildfowl, together with river deer, white whiskered boar and China hares.

Shooting weekends
Shooting weekends were a popular pastime with members of the British community in Shanghai during the late Victorian and the Edwardian periods. The more affluent sportsmen acquired houseboats to transport themselves by water along the Yangtze and some of its tributary rivers to the various destinations in the Yangtze Valley. Equipped with comfortable sleeping and dining accommodation, a kitchen, a lavatory, a secure gun and ammunition cabinet and gun dog kennels, such boats would be anchored offshore and left in the charge of the *lowdah* (skipper) while the owner, his guests and a team of *coolies* (crew members who also acted as beaters) disembarked in small tenders for the river bank and went out in pursuit of game. Shooting expeditions were invariably planned beforehand in great detail, with reference being made to the *Sportsman's Diary for Shooting Trips in North China*, the definitive guide to sport within reasonable reach of Shanghai.

Shooting party and Chinese attendants near Nanking, November 1921. Situated on the banks of the Yangtze river some 300 km from Shanghai and easily accessible by rail or steamer, Nanking (now known as Nanjing) was a popular destination for expatriate sportsmen during the late nineteenth and early twentieth centuries, many of whom were attracted by the superlative snipe bogs in the surrounding countryside

COOLIES AS BEATERS

Henling Thomas Wade offers the following advice on the deployment of houseboat coolies as beaters in *With Gun and Boat in the Yangtze Valley*:

'Coolies who are used as beaters and work well should be rewarded with a small *cumshaw* (gratuity), which should be given to them personally, not through the lowdah. After a long day's work at beating, especially in wet weather, a small quantity of spirits and water may be given to the beaters on their return to the boat. They will work all the better if they think that their exertions are appreciated, and will be rewarded. Never throw away an old pair of boots! Keep them until you go up-country, and then hand them over to the coolies employed as beaters. It is cruel to expect a coolie to work for hours at a time through covert, and over stubble, with nothing but straw shoes to protect his feet.'

Shooting in the Ningpo district

Some sporting destinations took only a couple of hours to reach; others might involve a journey of up to several days. Ningpo, for example, could be reached by steamer from Shanghai overnight or by houseboat within the space of a day. Shooting in the Ningpo district, according to a description given by H.P.Wadman in 1910:

'There is very fair shooting to be had at various spots around Ningpo, all easily accessible and within a night's journey of the port, but it is hardly a hunting ground a sportsman, whose chief aim was to make a big bag and who had plenty of time at his disposal, would choose, as, although there is plenty of game, the cover is too thick to work with much success with dogs. Five or six brace of pheasants in a day by a resident well acquainted with the country and a good shot is considered an exceptionally good bag. The charm of the shooting is the variety of game obtainable and the lovely country in which it is found, which is hilly and in most places thickly wooded. A certain number of hills are covered with scrub oak and dwarf fir trees amongst which the best pheasant shooting is to be had. Pheasants, partridges, deer and wild pig, &c., are all to be found in the adjacent hills, but the two latter are not often seen on account of the density of the cover which they frequent.'

Expatriate sportsmen and Chinese attendants posing for the camera just outside Nanking city walls, November 1921

Shooting in and around Shanghai and in the Yangtze Valley was undoubtedly at its peak between the 1870s and 1914. Notable bags taken during this period include 1,497 pheasants, 74 deer, 47 duck and teal, and 11 various taken by a party of six Guns in the Pejow district between 10 and 21 December 1873; 359 pheasants, 36 teal, 30 woodcock, 30 snipe, 20 quail, 18 duck, 2 deer and 6 various killed by Mr and Mrs Phelps Royall Caroll within the space of twenty-one full shooting and three half days at Wuhu in December 1891 (Mrs Caroll's gun was out of commission for a week during this period due to damage and had to be repaired by the armourer of *HMS Peacock* which happened to be in port at Wuhu); 540 pheasants shot over fourteen consecutive days at Wuhu in November 1901 by Mr Bell-Irving; and an extra large boar killed at Chinkiang on Christmas Day 1908 by Mr Rasmussen of the Customs Service which tipped the scales at 400 lbs.

NEW ZEALAND

I have resided for some years in the North Island, and have visited the South Island, and have no hesitation in saying that a settler who could spare the time would find plenty of rare birds, and might make a valuable collection. A sportsman would find wild ducks very numerous in both islands. The pukeko, or swamp hen, affords very good sport. The tui-tui, or mocking bird, and pigeons, both growing very fat, are in season at the beginning of winter. Quail are found in the South Island. In the interior, birds are numerous and tame; to a person accustomed to shoot over English fields the sport would seem very inferior. The mutton-bird, and a few others, are found on the sea-coast. The albatross keeps too far from land, but can be easily caught on the voyage to New Zealand. The wild pig is in parts plentiful, but soon deserts the settled districts, and after a time a settler must travel far from home for sport. It is generally hunted with dogs; an old boar at bay is an enemy not to be despised. A settler must not object to spend a night now and then among the natives, or at times to camp out in the bush. Gunpowder is hardly ever to be obtained good; very inferior stuff is 3/6d. (17½p) per pound; before purchasing it is necessary to have an order signed by the Resident Magistrate. – N.Z.

The Field 18 September 1858

TRAVEL TO THE
SHOOTINGS

GOING SHOOTING usually involves travel of some kind, be it simply driving to a host's house, a shoot room or a shooting lodge in order to shoot pheasants and partridges; journeying north by train to a Scottish sporting destination for grouse shooting, deer stalking and salmon fishing; or flying overseas to shoot partridges in Spain, big game in East Africa or duck in South America. In times past, Victorian and Edwardian sportsmen considered travel to be an integral part of any shooting expedition and happily endured a twenty-four hour journey by sleeper train, steamer and horse drawn carriage in order to reach a shooting lodge in the Outer Hebrides or the West of Ireland, or were quite prepared to undertake a long sea voyage to Africa or India for the purpose of big game shooting. These days sportsmen can drive from London to shoots in the West Country or East Anglia or fly to grouse moors and deer forests in far flung outposts of Scotland within the space of a few hours and can reach many of the major global sporting destinations by air within a day – essential for those with limited leisure time.

Arriving on the shooting field by rowing boat c. 1920

Travel from the shoot meeting point to the field has changed over the years, too. The sportsmen of yesteryear thought nothing of walking several miles in a day between stands or distant beats on a driven shoot or travelling to a remote grouse moor on horseback. On the more prestigious pheasant shoots, pony and trap or shooting brake transport was usually provided to convey Guns between distant beats and to the luncheon point. At Eaton Hall in Cheshire, shooting guests of the 2nd Duke of Westminster travelled from the hall to the afternoon stands by train on the estate's private narrow gauge railway, the locomotive often being driven by the duke himself. Rail travel was also used by Guns going to shoot grouse on Stanhope Moor in Co. Durham during the early years of the twentieth century. Apparently, the Guns were taken up to the moor in trucks which normally carried slag to the Consett Iron Works. Horse drawn shooting field transport was gradually replaced by motorised vehicles from the Edwardian period onwards and by the 1950s most estates were using Land Rovers, jeeps or ex-army lorries to convey parties of Guns. These, in turn, have been superseded by the Range Rover and other luxury four-wheel drive vehicles, together with pick-ups and ATVs. That said, quite a number of modern-day shoot operators now use early Land Rovers, vintage lorries and other classic vehicles as 'Gun buses' to convey sportsmen around the field.

Railway company advertisement for night sleeper services to Scotland 1937. Prior to the outbreak of World War Two in 1939, it was usual for sportsmen to travel to Scottish grouse moors by rail rather than by road

Sir Frederick Milbank, Bt. (standing beside pony), his gamekeepers and ghillies about to depart on a shooting and fishing expedition from Ardvourlie Castle, Isle of Harris 1865: courtesy of Sir Anthony Milbank, Bt.

Travelling to Scotland

Sportsmen first began to visit Scotland during the late eighteenth century, lured by the challenging grouse shooting and salmon fishing that could be obtained from Highland lairds, who charged little or nothing for the privilege. These early sporting tourists made the long journey north on horseback, by stage coach or by sailing boat, stopping off at inns or public houses en route for their nightly 'sleepover', and upon arrival at their destination lodged in a primitive inn, a farmhouse or a crofter's cottage for weeks or months on end. The sporting enthusiasts of the day continued to travel in this manner until the early 1820s when regular steam ship services were introduced between London and Leith and Glasgow and Inverness (via the Caledonian Canal), thus making it possible for an individual sportsman, his family and a retinue of servants or a group of Guns to reach the Highlands in relative comfort, and to make the onward journey to a shooting lodge in a hired carriage or by mail coach.

The age of the train

The steam ship was, in turn, replaced by rail travel, which enabled a sportsman and his entourage to journey north in a fast and comfortable overnight train from one of a number of London mainline stations. The railway reached Inverness in 1858, via a somewhat circuitous route from Aberdeen (this was followed by the opening of a more direct link via Perth in September 1863) and had arrived at the port of Strome Ferry on the west coast by 1870, providing easy access by sea to some of the principal deer forests and shootings in the Highlands and Islands. By 1881, it was possible to leave London at 8 in the evening and arrive at Perth by 8 a.m. on the following day – and to be at Inverness at 1.30 p.m. in time for lunch. Sportsmen travelling beyond Inverness invariably took a local stopping train to the nearest station to their shooting lodge, some of which had their own private halt.

TAKING THE TRAIN TO SCOTLAND IN THE 1890S

Colonel E.E.C. Hartopp describes rail travel to Scotland at the start of the grouse shooting season as it was in the early 1890s, in his book *Sport in England – Past and Present*, published in 1894:

'A casual person finding himself on the platform at Euston Station, from which the Scotch limited mail and its auxiliary will start about 8.40 pm during the first ten days of August, will be struck with all the bustle and commotion that takes place before these trains are despatched. If he is not a sportsman, he will naturally ask some porter what it all means. The reply will be that the crowd consists of gentlemen off to the moors to shoot grouse, in Scotland and elsewhere. On what kind of sport they are bent soon becomes self-evident: one glance of the eye at the nature of the luggage that is now coming along – the barrows are so heaped up that the porters who wheel them are not visible as they come towards you. There are gun cases and fishing-rod cases without end, to say nothing of the numerous boxes of early cartridges, which are no slight weight. Retrievers, and perhaps several brace of pointers and setters, are to be seen, nearly pulling the men's arms off who are leading them. I believe they know the time of year as well as human beings, also what is the "game."

In due course the trains start off on their long northern journey with all their living freight in the best of spirits. What a sudden calm now reigns on the platform! It gives a person time for reflection. This at once

THE
NORTH STAR,
STEAMER,
JAS. ANDERSON, Commander,
WILL SAIL

FROM INVERNESS FOR LONDON,
Calling off Cromarty, Invergordon, Burghead, and Banff,
(weather permitting), on
Monday, 14th August,...........at 2 o'clock afternoon.
Monday, 28th August,...........at 1 o'clock afternoon.

FROM LONDON,
Monday, 21st August,.............. 9 o'clock night.
Continuing (weather permitting) to sail every alternate Monday,
from Inverness and London, during the season.

Advertisement for the Inverness-London steamer service 1843

brings before you the rapid strides that have been made in the means of locomotion during the past forty years. Some of those sportsmen might have been bound for the very north of Scotland or the Island of Lewis, and they will arrive at their destination, even in the latter case, in the inside of two days' travelling.

The scene on the arrival of these trains at Perth Station is a thing never to be forgotten. Perth is a place where there are a great many junctions to all parts; this necessitates a great deal of changing and transhipment of baggage, &c. The platform is one mass of luggage and barking dogs, everybody is in a hurry, breaking their shins by tumbling over boxes, in the mad rush to get some breakfast (which I must say is first rate - what good butter and what good salmon cutlets!) before they renew the journey.

It is a perfect marvel that the baggage ever gets to its lawful owner. In ancient days this performance, say before the Highland line was made, or the northern extension of the Caledonian Railway, was chiefly done by coaching and steamboats after you had got as far as possible by rail. In fact, what then took a week can be done in two days now. All horses, carriages, dogs, servants, and heavy baggage used always to be sent round by sea, either to Aberdeen or Inverness, if their destination were near the east coast, if not, to some port on the West. And the shooting party made their way by coach with as little luggage as possible. But now, say August 12 falls on a Tuesday, a sportsman could start from London even as late as Sunday night, and might be rested and ready for the battle of the 12th on his moor.'

Travelling in style

Late Victorian and Edwardian sportsmen travelling to Scotland enjoyed the benefits of some of the best rail services in the country. Trains running between major stations not only offered fine dining facilities and luxurious sleeping accommodation, but conveyed a secure baggage van for housing guns, rifles and other necessary impedimenta and 'dog kennel' compartments during the sporting season. Most sportsmen reserved a couple of first-class compartments for their party and a third-class compartment for their servants when journeying north for the shooting season.

Rail travel to Scotland continued to be popular amongst members of the sporting fraternity up until the outbreak of World War Two in 1939, although by this time some men had started to make their annual pilgrimage to the north

Sportsmen about to depart for Scotland from Kings Cross Station,
London on 11 August 1904

Postcard issued to promote rail travel to Scotland for deer stalking enthusiasts c. 1930

by chauffeur-driven car or, indeed drove all the way themselves. Following the cessation of hostilities in 1945, the motor car gradually superseded the train as the preferred mode of travel to Scottish shootings. Sportsmen also started to take advantage of internal air services, travelling from London to Inverness, Aberdeen, Stornoway and other Scottish regional airports, using a hired car or a taxi for the final leg of their journey. That said, even today a few of the more traditional sporting types continue to travel north to their shooting quarters in style and comfort aboard the nightly Scotrail Caledonian Sleeper service from London Euston – affectionately dubbed the 'Deer Stalker Express'– which calls at nostalgic destinations as far afield as Corrour, Rannoch, Fort William, Gleneagles or Inverness.

Travelling to Ireland

Early sporting tourists travelled by mail coach from London and elsewhere to ports such as Holyhead or Liverpool, then made the onward journey across the Irish Sea by steamer or sailing ship to Dublin, Cork or Belfast before proceeding to their shooting quarters by carriage, jaunting car or on horseback. Things improved somewhat during the mid-Victorian period with the rapidly expanding rail network, which enabled sportsmen to take the boat-train from Euston to Holyhead or Stranraer, or from Paddington to Fishguard. From their port of arrival

SCOTTISH SPORTING ESTATE YACHTS

Considered to be an essential item of equipment on a Scottish island estate or an estate in a coastal location during the late Victorian and the Edwardian periods, the steam yacht was used to transport guests to and from the nearest railhead or seaport and to collect supplies for the shooting lodge, as well as to convey sportsmen to remote deer stalking and grouse shooting beats more accessible by sea than land. More often than not, yachts were the last word in luxury, having been built to the owner's personal specifications, and were crewed by experienced local sailors under the command of a professional sea captain. Sir Samuel Scott's yacht, for example, the 445 ton 106 h.p. *Golden Eagle*, built at Leith in 1899 for use at Amhuinnsuidhe Castle on the island of North Harris, boasted electric lighting – then something of an innovation – and sailed to South Africa during the Boer War to serve as a hospital ship.

Sporting estate yachts moored off Ballachulish, Argyll, September 1894.
Watercolour by Annie Winthrop

The Honourable Mr and Mrs Lockhart St. Clair leaving Dublin for the shootings in their Renault motor car c. 1905

they could catch a connecting train, travel by onward express from the nearest principal station to their final destination station and then continue their journey by horse drawn transport to their shooting lodge or hotel.

A long and arduous journey

Sportsmen, however, were often faced with a long and sometimes arduous journey from a country railway station to their shooting quarters prior to the arrival of the motor car in rural Ireland in the early 1900s, as T.P. Beaven a Wiltshire businessman, shot and angler recounts in his autobiography *A Sportsman Looks Back*:

> 'At Maam Cross Station we found our horse-driven side-car awaiting for us, and as I had eaten nothing since breakfast, I told my companions I intended to ask the stationmaster at this lonely wayside station if he could give me some bread and cheese. He was a very decent fellow, and gave me a pot of tea and an excellent meat pie, for which he would take no payment.
>
> We then started off on our sixteen-Irish-miles drive to Leenane. The horse was slow as he had already done twenty English miles meeting us. The hills were steep and long, so we were only too glad to get out and walk in order to stretch our legs and get some exercise. For miles after

leaving the station we did not pass a single house. The road ran up one hill and down another, and we were surrounded by endless chains of lochs, covered with duck of every description.

It was late in the evening before we reached Leenane Hotel – our destination. This is quite a good sized hotel on the Killary Bay, which is a large and broad arm of the sea which runs in for miles from the Atlantic, and is deep and wide enough for our Fleet to anchor in. As this is one of the beauty spots of Ireland, and the best centre for tourists doing Connemara, it was full of guests, among them many Americans and several fishermen.'

Superior connections for sportsmen

By the Edwardian era, it was possibly to leave Euston Station in London at 8.45 p.m. by the London & North Western Railway Irish Mail service, reach Dublin at 6.00 a.m. the following morning, depart from Broadstone Station in Dublin by the 7.00 a.m. Midland Great Western Limited Mail service bound for Westport in Co. Mayo – the principal station for many of the Mayo sporting estates – and arrive at 11.45 a.m., giving sportsmen the opportunity to shoot or fish in the afternoon or evening. For those travelling to the south-western counties of Ireland, on the Paddington to Rosslare overnight boat-train service via Fishguard, a special connecting express enabled anglers and shots to be out on the water or on the shooting field by 10 the next morning.

The rail-sea-rail boat-train service continued to be the principal mode of travel

Advertisement for Midland Great Western Railway Co. services to Connemara 1892. The company offered discounted fares to parties of sportsmen visiting the West of Ireland

to Irish sporting estates until the 1950s when sportsmen began to take cars by steamer to Ireland, or fly to regional airports and hire a car for the duration of their visit. Modern-day sporting visitors to the 'Emerald Isle' use one of the regular roll-on roll-off car ferry services; fly-drive packages, or travel to their destination by helicopter.

Travelling to Norway

British sporting tourists began to visit Norway during the mid-Victorian period, lured by superlative elk stalking, ryper and willow grouse shooting and salmon fishing. Travelling by scheduled steamer service from Hull to Bergen, Christiansund, Christiania (Oslo), Stavanger and other major seaports, the sportsmen of the day, then made an onward journey by steam launch, fishing boat or road to their shooting quarters, usually a hotel, a farmhouse or a purpose-built lodge. The voyage across the North Sea, which took around thirty-two to forty-eight hours to complete, was often rough and uncomfortable, requiring all but the most robust of passengers to remain in their cabins for the duration.

Cecil Braithwaite, a London stockbroker and a keen sportsman, who visited Norway to shoot and fish in 1897 records some details of such a journey in his book *Fishing Vignettes*:

> 'We started from Hull in a fog on board *SS Tasso*, a little tub of about 800 tons, and ran into a half-gale off the coast of Norway. So bad was it that one of our party was thrown out of her berth in the night, but fortunately was not much hurt. We arrived at Christiansund safely but late, and found that the little mail steamer which was to take us 40 miles up the fiord had started, so we chartered a small sort of half-decked steam boat, and after a most beautiful trip arrived at Sundal Soren, and were given a warm welcome by the inhabitants of the village.'

Price wise, the first-class return fare for travel aboard the *SS Tasso* from Hull to Christiansund at this time was in the region of £7. Under normal sea conditions, the *Tasso* operated by the Wilson Line (then the principal carrier to Norway) could complete the voyage to Christiansund in thirty-two hours, but often arrived late due to adverse weather conditions.

Overland by the rail-sea route

Travel to Norway became easier and more comfortable for sportsmen during the late 1890s with the inauguration of an overland rail-sea route from London to Norway via Harwich, Flushing, Hamburg and Copenhagen to Christiania (Oslo) which, apparently, conveyed luxurious sleeping carriages on the Hamburg to Christiania section. Sporting tourism was given a further boost in the early 1900s when Norwegian State Railways began to put on special trains prior to the start of each season to convey sportsmen and their equipment from many of the principal towns and seaports to stations in the main shooting and fishing areas. These trains often operated in conjunction with scheduled motor car 'bus' services which ran between stations and villages or hotels and shooting lodges and carried shooting and fishing parties to their final destination.

Christiania (now Oslo) Harbour c. 1880. Sporting tourists visiting Norway during the late Victorian period frequently travelled by steamer from Hull to Christiania, then made the onward journey to their shooting quarters by steam launch, fishing boat, rail or road

The rail-sea route from London to Norway continued to operate until 1914 when it was disbanded due to the outbreak of World War One. The Norwegian sporting tourist industry subsequently came to a standstill almost overnight owing to a lack of clientele, many of whom had taken up arms for the duration. Sadly overshooting and excessive netting during the war years ruined virtually all of the best game preserves and salmon rivers with the result that Norway ceased to be attractive to British sportsmen.

Travelling to India

In the early days of the Raj in the eighteenth century, travel from Great Britain to the Indian subcontinent was an arduous process involving a lengthy sea voyage via the Cape of Good Hope which might take at least six months to complete. This was often followed by an onward journey, sometimes of three or four months' duration, before the final destination, usually a military establishment or a major town, was reached.

From the 1830s onwards, the passage to India became easier with the opening of the Red Sea or Steam Route, which enabled members of the Raj and others to avoid the Cape of Good Hope by crossing the Mediterranean Sea to Alexandria, then to travel overland by horse drawn wagon and boat to Suez on the Red Sea, prior to making the final leg of the journey by East India Company paddle steamer from Suez to Bombay. This journey could be accomplished within around two months rather than six. The Red Sea Route was later shortened to around six weeks following construction of a railway linking Boulogne with Marseilles that made it possible for travellers to take the train from London to Folkestone, cross the Channel to Boulogne by packet steamer, then catch the luxurious Wagon-Lits express to the port of Marseilles in order to connect with the steamer service to Alexandria, thus avoiding the notorious swells and rollers of the Bay of Biscay. Travel conditions improved yet again in 1869 after the Suez Canal opened, which allowed steamers to sail directly to India via the Mediterranean Sea and the Red Sea (calling at Marseilles to collect passengers who had crossed France by rail) in less than a month.

The Indian Mail Service

The journey time from Great Britain to India was further reduced in 1871 with the inauguration of the weekly Indian Mail Service from London to Bombay via Brindisi in Italy, a rail-sea route which enabled senior members of the Raj and wealthy sportsmen to reach the subcontinent within the space of two weeks. The scheduled P&O Steamer service, which departed from Tilbury every Friday and sailed via Gibraltar and the Suez Canal to Bombay, took some three weeks

Advertisement for the P&O Steamship Co. 1905. Sportsmen, servicemen and administrators invariably travelled to India by P&O steamer. The SS Moldavia (pictured) operated on the England–Australia run from 1903 until the outbreak of World War One in 1914 and regularly called at Bombay (now Mumbai) en route

The Gateway to India, Bombay, opened in 1924. Sporting visitors to India during the late 1920s and the 1930s usually entered the country through the gateway upon disembarkation from their ship

to arrive at its destination at this time. Both of these services continued to operate until the outbreak of World War One.

Passenger and mail steamer services to India operated on a somewhat erratic basis for the duration of the war, crossing to the Suez Canal from the south of France instead of Italy. Thereafter, the scheduled weekly Indian Mail Service was reinstated but ran from London to Bombay via Marseilles rather than Brindisi, and continued to do so until the declaration of World War Two in 1939. By this time air travel from Great Britain to India had been introduced. It was utilised wherever possible by servicemen and members of the Raj throughout the war years and in the immediate post-war era, prior to India gaining independence in 1947. Since then sportsmen visiting India have invariably travelled by air rather than by sea.

The onward journey

Prior to the development of the Indian railway network during the second half of the nineteenth century, travel within India was frequently more time

consuming than the actual voyage out from Great Britain. Early sporting tourists
and soldiers or civilian administrators on leave happily journeyed great distances
in order to shoot or fish, accompanied by a large retinue of locally recruited
servants. Camping was the order of the day and many sportsmen spent two or
three months under canvas in the field while in pursuit of their quarry.

Organising a sporting expedition in India in the pre-railway era was not a
particularly difficult affair, though, according to an anonymous correspondent
writing in *The Field* in 1868:

> 'In India the country is either British, or under native chiefs, protected by
> or tributary to the Queen; locomotion is easy and not expensive, carts
> being almost everywhere procurable, or, failing carts pack bullocks or
> ponies. The country is studded with British cantonments 200 and 300
> miles apart, where supplies can be got to replenish the commissariat
> department, the traders' shops containing all things that may be desired,
> from Holloway's pills to moderator lamps, and Hall's gunpowder to bitter

Shooting camp in Srinagar, Kashmir c. 1910

beer and cod liver oil. With the exception of guns and rifles and their ammunition, an outfit for a six months sporting excursion might be got together in a day at any of the Presidency towns.'

Cost wise, our correspondent states that he calculates that the expenses incurred in going on a shooting visit to India during the autumn and winter months at this time, including travel from Great Britain: 'Would not be much more than taking a grouse moor for a season; certainly less than a deer forest'. He adds: 'If large game is shot in British Territory, the government rewards would considerably diminish the expenses. 50 rupees are given for tigers, 15 for panthers, 12 for bears and 5 for wolves or hyenas.'

Rail travel and improved roads

Late nineteenth and early twentieth century sportsmen in India benefited from rail travel and improved roads which enabled them to reach distant shooting grounds in far less time than previously, although the final part of the journey

Great Indian Peninsula Railway passenger express train about to depart from Bombay 1938. Having arrived in India by liner, sportsmen invariably made the next stage of their journey to the shootings by rail

very often involved a lengthy march on foot or horseback, especially if visiting places such as Ladakh, Baltistan or Nepal, all of which abounded with 'hill game'. Those travelling to the Himalayas to shoot, for example, could take the train as far as the city of Pathankhot in the northern state of Punjab, then hire a team of mules for the eight-day trek to Kailang in Lahaul, before reaching their final destination on foot, using yaks to carry camping kit and supplies. Expeditions of this nature, which involved a long march into the Himalayas, hard living, camping at 15,000 feet and rifle practice at big game rather than at fixed targets, were considered by the army 'top brass' of the day to be as good a training for young officers as an exercise with troops conducted under softer conditions.

Sportsmen, off-duty soldiers and civilian administrators could travel throughout India for very little cost during the days of the Raj and were able to cover hundreds of miles at a nominal figure, either by rail, horse drawn transport or on foot, assisted by hired coolies who could carry loads of up to 80 lb, or mules who could carry around 160 lb. Beaters and boats were readily obtainable in many areas as and when required, while a network of *dak* bungalows (government-owned guest houses for official travellers) along all of the major routes offered economical accommodation for those shooting or fishing in the surrounding district.

Travelling from Hong Kong to the Malay Peninsula

Some of the more adventurous soldiers and civilian administrators based in the colony of Hong Kong during the Victorian and the Edwardian periods spent their leave shooting big game on the Malay Peninsula. These intrepid sporting tourists happily made the long journey by sea from Hong Kong to Singapore, a distance of around 1,862 nautical miles, by steamer or cargo vessel then travelled to their chosen shooting grounds aboard a locally chartered boat.

Captain Edward Pennell-Elmhirst (1845–1916) of the 9th Regiment of Foot, who was stationed in Hong Kong during the early 1870s, provides us with a brief insight into the logistics of organising a sporting expedition to the Malay Peninsula at this time in these extracts from his diary (for an unspecified year) taken from his book *Foxhound, Forest and Prairie* published in 1892:

'Singapore, August 27 – Captain C. (a brother officer of the 9th.) and I with two months leave, have come down here to try for some shooting in the Malay Peninsula. We had a passage given us in one of Messrs. Jardine's steamers, or we could not well have managed it. Leaving Hong Kong on the 17th, we reached Singapore on the 25th. An eight days' voyage seemed rather a long one to undertake for the sake of shooting, but it is not so much for the shooting only, as to get away from Hong Kong for a time. We are going up country with Tuanko Solong, a Malay chief, and I believe, a great sportsman in his own way, and who happens to be just about to return to his own country for the elephant shooting. I must tell you the elephants come down from the hills at this time of the year, to feed on the corn and fruits in the plains, and there is more chance of bagging them now than at any other time. We have been obliged to spend a few days here to get things in readiness, buy provisions, &c., for our trip, in case game should be scarce.'

Elephant shooting on the Malay Peninsula. Coloured aquatint by J. Marshman c. 1870s

'August 30 – We start at daylight to-morrow morning; and have to go about eighty miles up the west coast to meet the mouth of the Maor river, which flows into the sea close to Malacca. We then turn up the river to get to our shooting ground, so shall not be able to begin work until Sept. 2 or 3, instead of the 1ˢᵗ, as I should have liked. We have hired a big boat of about 11 tons, called a tongkong, for our expedition. This requires five men, and will either sail or can be rowed. Her cost is a dollar a day. We shall have lots of room in her, which will be a great comfort, as we shall have to live almost entirely on board. I am taking my Chinese boy to cook for us, and C. has engaged a Malay servant who can act as interpreter, for Mr Tuanko speaks nothing but his native gibberish. We have a good deal to do in the way of getting steel tips made for bullets, and a thousand and one little necessaries. We are going into a very good game country, and certainly ought to get sport of some kind, either in the shape of elephant, buffalo, or deer, though it will be a great chance if we get a shot at a tiger in that part of the peninsula.'

'September 6 – We left Singapore on the 31ˢᵗ August in the tongkong, our party consisting of Captain C. and myself, Tuanko Solong, the young Rajah of Johore – a great swell in his own country, five Malay boatmen, two gun carriers, both well tried fellows, and my Chinese boy as cook, &c. We had part of our boat covered with mats, and secured ourselves a dry sleeping place in all weathers. Moving along the west coast of Johor, for about eighty miles, we reached the mouth of the Moar river on Sunday, Sept. 3. The scenery among the islands in the straits of Malacca is very beautiful; the land is covered with splendid green forest reaching down to the very edge of the water. The next day we moved a few miles up the river, which is around 500 yards across in this part; secured two guides, old hands at elephant tracking; landed and went out for an hour or two. Here we had our first experience of what the Malay jungle is to move through. The whole country is much the same, being one huge forest, with a dense undergrowth of thorny jungle of different kinds; and generally speaking, a knee-deep swamp under foot, with the pleasure of floundering up to your fork occasionally in the holes made by the elephants' feet. It is necessary always to have a man in front to clear the way with his parang (heavy knife). Of course, this day found us terribly out of commission, and returned to the boat about two o'clock regularly beat, and without having seen anything, though we heard that five

Pig shooting party, Elmina estate, Selangor, Malay Peninsula, 10 September 1950

elephants had been close to the huts of the natives, on the bank of the river, during the previous night. The people brought us some fowls, wild honey, and sugarcane for sale. Before going any further, I must tell you of our daily routine during the trip. Up at daylight; buckets of water poured over us on deck; a light breakfast, consisting of a cup of coffee and a biscuit, with a glass of sherry and quinine to keep off jungle fever (which I am glad to say it did from both of us during the whole five weeks we spent in the jungle); land and work till between twelve and two pm; then return to the boat, wash, change, clean our guns, and sit down to the meal of the day with an enormous appetite; this over about three generally, we smoke, talk and loll about till dark (unless we go on shore again); then some soup, &c.; after that a smoke, put up mosquito curtains, and turn in about eight o'clock.'

LADIES ON THE
SHOOTING FIELD

GAME SHOOTING has become increasingly attractive to members of the fairer sex in recent years, prompting much comment in the sporting press on the subject of ladies on the shooting field. In some circles, the presence of a female in a line of Guns is still considered to be somewhat innovative despite the fact that ladies in the British Isles first took up shooting during the mid-Victorian period, several years before the American celebrity shot, Annie Oakley, was born.

Sporadic press reports carried by regional rather than national newspapers indicate that ladies had certainly started to take an interest in shooting by the late 1850s. For example, in 1857, the *Nottingham Review* observed:

Alma, Marchioness of Breadlebane, with a grassed stag

'Melton Mowbray can boast of three public characters which perhaps no other town can – namely two independent ladies who have taken out game certificates, and who can enter the field and can bring down the game equal to any male sportsman, as well as those indulging in fishing, hunting over a country to hounds, &c. The other is a female blacksmith, who is such an adept at shoeing a horse, or working at the anvil, as to cause universal admiration.'

Ladies, however, are rarely mentioned in game books and other shoot records until the early 1860s, usually shooting grouse and stags on Highland sporting estates rather than going out in pursuit of pheasants and partridges on low ground shoots in England and Wales. Many of these daring sportswomen, who defied Queen Victoria's edict that 'only fast women shot', were also keen anglers, fishing for salmon and sea trout in well-known rivers.

The early female shots came from a variety of backgrounds ranging from Alma, Marchioness of Breadlebane, the aristocratic wife of a major Scottish landowner, to Jessie Thorneycroft, the daughter of a wealthy Black Country ironmaster, who shot her first stag in Glen Tanar in Aberdeenshire in 1865 aged just seventeen years. Almost without exception each lady was something of a character, prepared to spend a day out in the field or on the hill wearing tweeds in pursuit of her quarry, in the company of gentlemen, gamekeepers and ghillies, yet able to look her best in an evening dress at dinner in the evening.

Shooting remained very much a minority sport amongst ladies during the 1870s and '80s but by the 1890s had gained in popularity, particularly in aristocratic circles. The fashion houses of the day, quick to take advantage of this growing trend, designed smart woollen shooting costumes with matching caps for lady shots, and even produced attire suitable for wearing on a grouse moor consisting of tweed knickerbockers, a matching knee length coat and cap, and special boots and stockings.

*Edwardian postcard depicting a
smartly dressed lady shot*

*Guns and their ladies enjoying a picnic lunch on the grouse moor
at Castle Leod, Ross-shire 1903*

Lady Sophie Scott wearing typical shooting attire for the Edwardian lady

SHOOTING LADIES

Lady Mildred Boynton (presumably a lady shot) has this to say about the growing interest in shooting amongst females during the early 1890s in *Ladies in the Field*, published in 1894:

'A few years ago a 'shooting-lady' was almost as much a *rara avis* as the Great Auk; if here and there one member of the sex, more venturesome than her fellows, were bold enough to take to the gun in preference to the knitting needle, she was looked upon as most eccentric and fast, and underwent much adverse criticism. Now, however, *nous avous change tout cela*. Ladies who shoot, and who shoot well, too, are springing up on all sides, and the clamour raised by their appearance is gradually subsiding. There are still dissentient voices here and there, it is true, voices which proclaim aloud that women have no place in the covert and among the turnips, and that the cruelty of the sport should be an insuperable objection to their joining in it. A discussion of all the pros and cons is, however, outside the scope of these notes, we simply have to deal with the facts as they stand, and, undoubtedly, the "shooting-lady" is now as much an established fact as is her sister the 'hunting-woman.'

Those women of the period who felt that shooting was not a ladylike activity nevertheless usually showed some enthusiasm for the sport by joining their menfolk for luncheon on the field, a lavish affair held in a marquee, a purpose built luncheon lodge or al fresco style. Thereafter, it was the custom for the ladies to accompany the Guns and their loaders as spectators during the afternoon drives. It was not unknown for a particularly adventurous lady to tramp through the heather and squeeze into a grouse butt alongside her husband and his loader after a hearty lunch on the moors.

By the Edwardian era, ladies had become a relatively common sight on the shooting field, although they were rarely seen in a top line of Guns at a large shooting party. Leading lady shots at this time include Lady Juliet MacCalmont, Mrs Willie Jameson, who specialised in partridge shooting, and Hilda Murray of Elibank, an all-round sportswoman whose activities included shooting, hunting and fishing.

The lady landowners of the day, although pretty thin on the ground, were invariably keen shots. Maude Cheape, Master of the Bentley Harriers, who owned estates in Worcestershire, Warwickshire and on the Isle of Mull, preserved game on all of her properties and participated in the pheasant and partridge shoots that she organised for her friends, preferring one hundred bird days to big bags. Although she reared a large number of pheasants on her Bentley Manor estate, she expected her gamekeepers to maintain a good stock of foxes and hares at all times. Indeed, when engaging a new head keeper named Cox, she gave him the following warning: 'Remember, no fox, no Cox!'

There were a handful of lady sporting lessees, too. Mary, 11th Duchess of Bedford, for example, known as the 'Flying Duchess' for her pioneering aviation exploits, was not only a keen ornithologist but also a remarkable shot. She leased the shooting rights over part of the island of Barra in the Outer Hebrides during the late Edwardian period in order that she could combine bird watching with game shooting, travelling north annually aboard the ducal yacht, the *Sapphire*. Being of a practical nature and keen on shooting in comfort, she shocked her peers by suggesting that shooting skirts should be 'no longer than eight inches below the knee'.

Shooting was by no means limited to upper class Edwardian ladies, though. There were several lady gamekeepers employed on sporting properties in various parts of the country – at least one of whom was reputed to be a crack-shot – as

Lady shot with a rabbit for the pot 1904

Maude Cheape, Master of the Bentley Harriers; one of the few lady shoot owners during the Edwardian era

well as a lady head gamekeeper, Mary Bayman, who managed a team of three under-keepers on the Poynters estate in Surrey. It goes without saying, of course, that there were lady poachers around, too, some of whom no doubt knew how to handle a gun.

Ladies who shot were not always popular with Edwardian sporting gentlemen or gamekeepers, however, many of whom actively discouraged females from taking up the gun or rifle. One correspondent writing in *The Gamekeeper* in October 1902 advised his fellow keepers to add a little extra black powder to the cartridges if teaching a young lady to shoot as this would produce a bruise like effect on her shoulder which would deter her from wearing a low cut ballgown and, thus, discourage her from wishing to shoot again. The same correspondent, who wrote under the pseudonym of 'A Very Old Keeper', went on to share his experiences of dealing with lady shots with readers of the magazine:

Obviously keen to solicit business from lady shots, cartridge manufacturers Eley Bros placed this advertisement in the sporting press in 1911

'I have never yet known a lady to join a shooting party as an active participator without thoroughly upsetting it, so I only hope those with longings that way will confine their presence to the lunch table only. First of all she can never refrain from engaging the sportsmen in conversation at all kinds of inopportune moments, to the irritation of the elder ones and amusement of the younger. When the party is asked to pass silently along a ride, her stage whispers are more alarming to game than the voice would be if used in the ordinary way, and she can never stand quietly and wait the coming of game. The interval between the posting of the Guns and the appearance of the game is bound to be whiled away by conversation, shouted to and fro, or else she will decoy some young and impressible fellow from his place to talk. She forgets that Guns nearly always act as stops, and that the removal of one from his allotted position may have the effect of spoiling the whole beat. The sportswoman's desire to talk is really her greatest drawback, and if she would get over this, I, as a keeper, would try and endure the rest of her faults. She generally arrives late at the appointed place, and this exasperates everyone, and then will persist in handing her dainty little breech loader round for all to admire. This causes further delay, as there is sure to be some amongst the party anxious to admire her gun, and everything else which is hers, in the hope of getting a little back in return. I find the best way to hurry matters is to stalk off with the beaters, and then this gives the Guns an excuse for moving on too.'

Following the outbreak of World War One, the majority of lady shots laid down their guns to become voluntary nurses in 'country house' hospitals for wounded soldiers or carried out other important tasks allocated to females by the military authorities. A few continued to be involved in shooting, however, either going out with a gun in pursuit of rabbits, hares or pheasants to augment their wartime rations or working as temporary gamekeepers on sporting estates.

After the cessation of hostilities in 1918, the interest in shooting sadly declined amongst younger members of the fairer sex, many of whom preferred the more glamorous London lifestyle of the 'bright young things' of the 1920s rather than Edwardian country living. Other than a minority of 'outdoor' girls who eschewed the Metropolis in favour of hunting, shooting and fishing in the countryside, the only young ladies who continued to shoot at this time

Elsie Reeves who worked as a temporary gamekeeper on the Whatcombe estate in Dorset during World War One

Lady and gentlemen Guns taking a breather on the grouse moor, Ullinish, Isle of Skye 1925

tended to be wealthy enthusiasts who generally shot alongside their husbands, either on his own shoot or as an invited guest on a friend's estate. The latter included Mrs Hugh Corbet, the wife of a Shropshire squire, an all-round sportswoman who was equally at home on grouse moor, partridge manor or pheasant shoot; the 9th Viscountess Powerscourt a well-known poet and a superlative grouse shot (considered by Lord Home of the Hirsel to be the leading lady shot of her day); Sybil, 5th Marchioness of Cholmondley, whose husband owned the celebrated Houghton Hall shoot in Norfolk; Mrs Enid Gore, reputed to be the first woman to shoot grouse from a butt in Wales; and the exotic Mrs Elita Philippi, the daughter of a Chilean diplomat who was married to the celebrated shot, Colonel George Philippi of Crawley Court in Hampshire and competed against her husband at Wilton, Broadlands, Six Mile bottom and other prestigious English shoots.

The ladies' shooting scene of the 1920s and '30s was very much dominated by older women, some of whom had taken up the sport during the Victorian period. Mary, 11th Duchess of Bedford, for example, bagged a total of 273 'remarkably tall' pheasants with 366 cartridges on the family estate at Woburn Abbey on 31 January 1923 and once killed 84 pheasants at one stand using 96 cartridges. Lady Arthur Grosvenor who, apparently, often travelled to country house shoots in her gipsy caravan, shot pheasants with a Purdey 20 bore gun and reversed roles with her loader during afternoon drives.

Quite a number of the elderly lady shots of the day were deer stalking enthusiasts, too. Lady Evelyn Cobbold, who owned the 14,500 acre Glen Carron Deer Forest, a superlative stalker and angler, also became a convert to Islam and was the first English woman to make the pilgrimage to the holy city of Mecca in Saudi Arabia, undertaking the journey at the age of sixty-six in 1933. Lady Sophie Scott, an accomplished all-round stalker, game shot and salmon fisher, who was the first lady to successfully catch trout on the Houghton Club waters of the river Test in Hampshire, accounted for a total bag of 698 red deer on the Amhuinnsuidhe estate on the Isle of Harris between 1919 and the time of her death in 1937. She chose to be buried in a specially built mausoleum in the Amhuinnsuidhe Deer Forest. Last but not least, there was the redoubtable Mrs Jessie Platt, proprietor of the 42,000 acre Eishken estate on the Isle of Lewis, who spent in excess of six months of each year pursuing red deer, grouse, salmon and other game at her Outer Hebridean sporting retreat and notched up something of a record in Scottish sporting circles, having shot and stalked continuously for seventy seasons prior to her death in February 1935 at the advanced age of eighty-six years.

When World War Two was declared in 1939, the majority of the surviving lady shots were getting on in years and were considered too old for gamekeeping or defence duties. Shooting, however, continued to be carried out by gamekeepers' wives and daughters, who had often learned to handle a gun surreptitiously, and now came into their own, protecting game preserves from vermin while their husbands were away in the armed services.

Some of the more progressive ladies of the immediate post-war era began to take up game shooting during the late 1940s and early 1950s, and were usually welcome guests on shoots owned by enlightened landowners such as Earl Mountbatten of Burma. Deborah, Duchess of Devonshire, and the Countess of Brecknock and Lady Sopwith, both of whom smoked pipes on the shooting field, were all noted characters in female shooting circles at this time.

Other than on a number of family shoots, where wives and daughters were encouraged to learn to shoot in order that they could join their menfolk on an equal footing on the shooting field rather than as spectators, game shooting

LADY SHOTS FROM OVERSEAS

Notwithstanding the relative lack of enthusiasm for game shooting in female circles for much of the Victorian period, a steady trickle of European lady shots visited Great Britain every year as invited guests on British sporting estates, often to shoot red grouse rather than pheasants or partridges. Princess Pelagia Radiwill, for instance, the wife of a Polish nobleman, shot regularly with Sir Frederick Milbank, Bt., at Barningham Park in North Yorkshire. The more adventurous French Baroness de Veauce travelled to the Isle of Lewis in the Outer Hebrides from time to time for challenging walked-up grouse shooting. These European female sporting tourists were later joined by ladies from the elite of American society during the early twentieth century, many of whom crossed the Atlantic by liner annually with their husbands and families in order to shoot red grouse in England or Scotland, a tradition which has continued to the present time, albeit on a limited scale.

Mrs Guinevere Gould, wife of the American millionaire and railway king George J. Gould, shooting grouse on a Scottish moor, August 1922

continued to be something of a low key activity amongst members of the fairer sex as late as the 1970s. Indeed commenting on the situation in her book *A Countrywoman's Year* published in 1973, Georgina Rose, one of the relatively few lady shots of the period (and the daughter of well-known shots, Colonel George and Mrs Elita Philippi) states:

> 'Women shooting is still an emotive subject. Shooting is a man's world, and any girl who enjoys the sport has to tread carefully. Women's Lib. would find it a fruitful field in which to exercise their activities, although heaven forbid that they should try. Men and women go stalking and fishing on equal terms, but shooting game with a shot gun can still produce quite violent male prejudice, which is dying hard, if at all. My mother, in the twenties and thirties, had notable contemporaries, but there is no increase in the number of women shots of my age and there appear to be even fewer of the children's.'

Since the late 1970s game shooting has become an increasingly popular sport with women, helped undoubtedly by the rapid growth in commercial shooting over the past few decades which has made it possible for a woman to participate at a shoot as a paying Gun in an unbiased environment. Further, during this period the number of lady gamekeepers employed on British sporting estates has increased from less than half a dozen to in excess of one hundred, while lady beaters

Lady Gun in action on a ladies' shooting day at Ripley Castle, North Yorkshire, January 2013: courtesy of Hurworth Photography/ www.hurworth-photos.co.uk

Girl power: team of lady Guns on a ladies' shooting day at Ripley Castle, North Yorkshire, January 2014: courtesy of Hurworth Photography/ www.hurworth-photos.co.uk

(some of whom shoot), once something of a rarity, can now be found on many shoots working alongside their male counterparts.

Today, shooting is no longer the exclusive privilege of the rich and the famous but is open to ladies from all walks of life, either as invited guests on private shoots, as paying Guns on commercial shoots or through female shooting societies such as the Dorset Game Birds, the Devon & Somerset Ladies Shooting group, the Just for Ladies Shooting Club and the Shotgun & Chelsea Bun Club. If game shooting is to survive in the twenty-first century on a positive note, it is vital that more and more members of the fairer sex become involved in the sport and are treated with the respect that they deserve by male Guns and members of the gamekeeping fraternity.

MRS ELITA PHILIPPI – LADY SHOT

One of the most notable lady shots during the 1920s and '30s, Elita Philippi was born in 1897, the youngest daughter of Don Julio de Bittencourt of the Chilean Legation in London. She began her shooting career in World War One while staying on the Crosswood estate in West Wales, home of her brother-in-law and sister, the Earl and Countess of Lisburne. Finding little to do on a lengthy holiday at Crosswood, she purchased a 20 bore gun and spent her days out in the field in pursuit of rabbits. She subsequently took up game bird shooting in the immediate post-war period, honing her gunnery skills on a relative's property in Spain.

Following her marriage to the well-known shot, Colonel George Philippi in 1922, Elita quickly discovered that she would need to take up shooting as a pastime on a more or less full-time basis if she was to see her husband at all during the shooting season. In order to compete with him on an equal footing as an invited guest on the many shoots that he attended, she acquired a pair of Purdey shot guns, took shooting lessons from an instructor at the West London Shooting School and enlisted Mr Graves, the family chauffeur, as her loader. Such was her enthusiasm for

the sport that in the late 1920s and the early 1930s, according to her son Robert, she purchased between 20,000 and 22,000 cartridges from Purdeys annually!

From the mid-1920s until the outbreak of World War Two in 1939, Elita and George regularly shot on their own estate at Crawley Court in Hampshire and on a section of the Wilton estate which they rented from the Earl of Pembroke, as well as at Highclere, Six Mile Bottom, Broadlands and many other well-known English pheasant and partridge shoots. They opened the season in Scotland on 12 August every year, shooting grouse at Ardverikie, Giack and elsewhere in the Highlands before heading south to shoot grouse at Keld, Gunnerside and on other northern moors, returning to Crawley just in time to shoot partridges on 1 September. Having spent a few weeks partridge shooting at Crawley, the Philippis travelled back to Scotland for more grouse shooting, then returned to England in October for pheasant shooting. In addition to shooting grouse in Scotland, Elita often went out deer stalking, something which she proved to be remarkably adept at – unlike her husband, who was not too keen on rifle shooting.

Elita rented the Compton shoot near

Stockbridge in Hampshire for one season during the 1930s in order to entertain guests in her own right, but things did not work out as her husband and his friends soon took charge of the operation for their own benefit. She later ran a rough shoot on the Crawley estate during the Second World War when her husband was away serving in the RAF, leaving the organisation to a soldier billeted in the house who had previously been a notorious poacher.

In the aftermath of the war, Elita and her husband not only shot at Crawley but leased the Broadlands shoot at Romsey from Earl and Countess Mountbatten of Burma for some years in order to provide additional shooting facilities. She subsequently acquired her own shoot in Spain following George's death in 1953, continuing to take a keen interest in the sport until old age forced her to give up.

Elita Philippi died in 1980. Her son Robert and daughter Georgina both became noted shots in their own rights. Georgina, who learnt to shoot as a girl, was in fact one of the few ladies to be present on the shooting 'circuit' from the late 1940s until the early 1980s, when shooting started to become popular amongst women.

Mrs Elita Philippi (holding gun) on a visit to Spain c. 1922: courtesy of Mrs G. Rose

GAME SHOOTING DURING
THE GREAT WAR

SPORTSMEN WERE AMONGST THE FIRST TO VOLUNTEER their services to fight for King and country when Great Britain declared war against Germany on 4 August 1914. Many were already serving officers in territorial battalions of county regiments or were retired army or naval officers who had invariably fought in armed conflicts in the colonies or had spent time in India. All experienced shots had kept up their gunnery skills on the great Edwardian pheasant and partridge shoots, on the grouse moors, in the deer forests of Scotland and on big game shooting expeditions overseas.

Gilbert Holmes, a keen sportsman and enthusiastic piper who turned down a commission in a Guards regiment to serve as private soldier in the regimental pipe band of the Seaforth Highlanders during the Great War: courtesy of the Holmes family

Soldier-sportsmen

Unsurprisingly a remarkable number of these soldier-sportsmen left for the front accompanied by a shot gun and a light fishing rod, anticipating that they would be able to shoot or fish during any free time that they might have. Some also took along their valet, their chauffeur or a gamekeeper to act as their 'batman' (personal servant), to undertake loading duties as and when necessary and to care for their sporting equipment.

Notwithstanding the fact that game shooting and hunting had been banned in France by the French Government at the beginning of the war and had been prohibited by the British military authorities in 1915, many soldier-sportsmen managed to engage in sporting activities in the French countryside and elsewhere with the blessing of senior officers whenever they had a day or two to spare, often organising an impromptu shoot using former gamekeepers serving in the ranks as loaders and other soldiers as beaters. Geoffrey Dent, an officer in the 4th Dragoon Guards, often went out in pursuit of hares and partridges on horseback, shot at boar, woodcock, duck and rats and had a go at badger digging in his 'rest periods' before returning to shoot at the enemy. Lieutenant Eric Harrison of the Royal Artillery, while stationed in France on staff duties, rode after partridges and hares on free afternoons which, apparently, could be chased to the point of exhaustion and picked-up by hand. Colonel Lewis Carey, who served in France from 1914 until 1916, not only shot partridges illicitly for the table for his GOC and for the local district Mayor, but also put his gun to good use bringing down German carrier pigeons in order to intercept enemy messages. Lt. Colonel Lord Dorchester, who was based at GHQ in Salonika from 1916 until 1918, regularly went on woodcock shooting expeditions in the Macedonian countryside during the season accompanied by an ADC, an orderly and a small kennel of dogs, using a staff car for transport.

Sportsmen Home on Leave

Sportsmen home on leave and those permanently based in Great Britain on troop training or guard duties were able to continue shooting on a regular basis during the season for the greater part of the war. They used soldiers who had

Soldier-sportsmen posing with the day's bag taken on a rabbit shoot 1915

been gamekeepers as loaders, and land girls or German prisoners of war as beaters. Indeed, according to some sources, off-duty officers and gentlemen too aged or decrepit to be useful on the battlefield were encouraged by the authorities to carry on with the annual slaughter of pheasants, partridges and grouse in order to provide nourishing meals for soldiers in hospitals and convalescent homes and to augment the food supplies for towns and cities.

SHOOTING ON THE STOKE PARK ESTATE, IPSWICH

September 15th, 4 Guns, 31 brace partridges, 1 hare, 2 rabbits; September 21st, 5 Guns, 46 brace partridges, 2 hares, 2 rabbits; all the Guns being officers in khaki, some of them have now gone to the Dardanelles for bigger game.

A. Cousins, head gamekeeper
The Gamekeeper October 1915

Contemporary Game Books

Contemporary game books indicate that shooting continued unabated on some estates, albeit on a smaller scale than in pre-war years due to gamekeeping and beating staff shortages caused by the hostilities. On the Elveden estate in Suffolk a total of 18,394 pheasants and 2,872 partridges were shot by Lord Iveagh and his friends during the course of the 1914 shooting season. At Broadlands in Hampshire, Lt. Colonel Wilfred Ashley, MP, and his guests brought down 905 pheasants, 588 partridges and 173 duck, plus small numbers of hares, woodcock and other game in 1915. At

Off-duty airmen on a deer shooting expedition c. 1918

Eishken on the Isle of Lewis in the Outer Hebrides, one of the larger Scottish deer forests, off-duty officers and other guests accounted for 85 stags, 74 hinds, 365 red grouse (walked-up) and 365 hares in 1915. While on the renowned Wemmergill grouse moor in Teesdale, the lessee and various invited Guns took an above average bag of 7,108 red grouse (driven) in 1916.

Seasonal game bag records for the various quarry species appear not to have been kept on a national basis during the war years other than for deer which came under the jurisdiction the Venison Supply Committee. The Committee allocated supplies of venison to the Admiralty and the War Office. In 1916, for example, sportsmen and stalkers shooting in the Scottish deer forests and the English deer parks accounted for a total of 18,832 beasts, weighing an aggregate of 2,186,000 lb.

Game Preservation and Shooting

Game preservation and shooting, surprisingly, remained untouched until a government order implemented in 1917 under the terms of the Defence of the Realm Act made it a criminal offence to use grain and other foodstuffs for game bird rearing. The order also temporarily extended the grouse shooting season from 6 August to 20 January to enable a greater number of birds to be shot for food purposes; allowed farmers to shoot any game birds that came on to their land to prevent crop damage; and to enter adjoining woodlands or moors to cull rabbits for the same purpose.

Shooting was dealt a further blow in 1918 when the Ministry of Food imposed a rationing system which prohibited sportsmen, gamekeepers and others from purchasing more than a stated number of shotgun and rifle cartridges. Game supplies were restricted, too, with books of ration coupons being issued to landowners, employees and regular gift recipients limiting the amount of game from a shoot that could be kept for personal consumption in order to ensure that the bulk of the bag went into the national food supply chain via a game dealer. However, rabbits and hares were ration-free if shot by an individual solely for household use.

SOLDIERS AS SPORTSMEN

Colonel Alfred Gilbey, who raised the Bucks Territorial Battalion of the Oxfordshire & Bucks Light Infantry in 1915, considered it to be necessary for his officers to gain some experience in the use of the shot gun during their training period to augment their rifle skills:

'I had the honour of raising and commanding a Territorial battalion, and any success I had was due to the fact that I encouraged in every possible way the sporting instincts of my officers and men. During the first summer we were encamped in Lord Lincolnshire's Park at High Wycombe. He was kind to give us the shooting over his estate. What fun we had those Saturday afternoons in September and October! Though all my officers were well qualified to give instruction with the rifle, I had no experience as to their prowess with the shot gun, and therefore I felt it was necessary to give them a certain amount of instruction, and they clearly understood that if any of them fired a dangerous shot or followed round it would mean being sent back to camp in disgrace. However, I never had to put this into force. The shooting may have been a bit erratic, but no accident happened, and the bugle boys who acted as beaters enjoyed themselves as much as the Guns. I warrant his lordship never had more appreciative guests. Three of those who took part in the sport had given up permanent and lucrative positions in Ceylon to join the Army, and, alas, all three of them were killed on the Somme the following year!'

Sadly, a large number of sportsmen lost their lives fighting for their country on the battlefields of Europe, on the high seas or in the air, amongst them some of the finest shots in Great Britain. Those that returned were hit by the high taxation imposed by the Lloyd George Liberal Government following the cessation of hostilities in 1918, which not only meant that many shoot owners were obliged to reduce their landholdings and lay off staff and in some cases to run a walked-up rather than a driven shoot, but that wealthy sporting tenants from the financial and industrial sectors could often no longer afford to rent low ground pheasant and partridge shoots, grouse moors or Scottish deer forests. Shooting would never be quite the same again.

GAMEKEEPERS OF THE FIRST SPORTSMEN'S BATTALION (23rd ROYAL FUSILIERS)
Grey Tower Barracks, Hornchurch, Essex.

Standing (from left to right).

		EMPLOYER.
1.	Sergt. D. F. ROBERTSON	The Right Hon. Lord Kinnaird, Rossie Priory, Perthshire.
2.	Piper D. SEATH	J. Martin White, Esq., Ballruddery, Perthshire.
3.	Pte. M. RIDDELL	Sir Hugh Shaw Stewart, Bart., Carnock, Larbert, N.B.
4.	Pte. W. ION	Admiral Johnstone Stewart, Glassington, Wigtonshire.
5.	Pte. H. McGREGOR	The Right Hon. Lord Kinnaird, Rossie Priory, Perthshire.
6.	Pte. JAS. McFARLANE	J. Hunting, Esq., Slaley Hall. Northumberland.

Sitting (left to right).

1.	Pte. T. BRYDEN	D. Kerr, Esq., Martin Hall, Newton Stewart, N.B.
2.	Pte. R. CRABB	A. P. Lyle, Esq., Glendelvine, Murthly, Perthshire.
3.	Pte. ROBERT HANNAH	The Right Hon. Earl of Galloway, Cumloden, Newton Stewart, N.B.
4.	Pte. J. CARNOCHAN	W. M. Neilson, Esq., Barcaple, Kirkcudbright.

		EMPLOYER.
7.	Pte. FOGGO	Lord Blythswood, Blythswood House, Renfrew.
8.	Piper A. McLENNAN	Earl Fitzwilliam, Shillelagh, Co. Wicklow.
9.	Pte. J. MUIRHEAD.	W. Hodgson, Esq., Fairgirth, Kirkcudbright.
10.	Pte. J. WILSON	Duke of Athole, K.T., Blair Castle, Perthshire.
11.	Pte. J. McFARLANE	J. W. Oxley, Esq., Penninghame, Wigtonshire.
12.	Piper WM. JOHNSTONE	J. W. Oxley, Esq., Penninghame, Wigtonshire.
13.	Corp. Piper McCLUNIE	The Hon. Thomas Cochrane, Crawford Priory, Fifeshire.

5.	Sergt. SCHOFIELD	Colchester Garrison, Shooting Syndicate.
6.	Pte. G. R. GIBSON	The Right Hon. Earl of Galloway, Cumloden, Newton Stewart, N.B.
7.	Pte. H. McARDLE	Errwood, Buxton, Derbyshire.
8.	Pte. P. FERGUSON	A. Dawson, Esq., The Fountainhall and Woodhall Shootings, Pencaitland, East Lothian.

Gamekeepers of the 1st Sportsmen's Battalion, 23rd Royal Fusiliers. The Battalion was formed in London in September 1914 and consisted principally of sportsmen, adventurers and gamekeepers

SHOOTING
TUITION

SHOOTING TUITION was traditionally carried out by the head gamekeeper on a country estate who would be entrusted to give his employer's sons lessons in gun handling, marksmanship, fieldcraft, vermin control and other relevant subjects. From the age of ten years onwards, sometimes a little earlier, a boy would go out with him bolting and shooting rabbits, an exercise which also involved studying wind direction, learning to stand perfectly still and working in silence. Thereafter, he would graduate to walked-up partridge shooting and, eventually, start to accompany the head keeper on pheasant shooting expeditions around the estate boundaries (to supply birds for the kitchens) before being allowed to join his father and his guests on small driven days by the time that he had reached his late teens.

Gamekeeper (right) and boy shot with the day's bag c. 1920s

LEARNING TO SHOOT – 1870s STYLE

'My course of instruction continued from the age of fourteen until I reached my majority, all my holidays being practically devoted to it, and well do I remember my pride on overhearing the keeper confide to my father that he believed me destined to become quite a good shot. It was indeed a day of days when in early October I stood at the end of an outlying plantation, with my parents looking on, while the keeper and his dog beat it towards me. I was on trial, to decide if my skill and deportment warranted my joining a shooting party proper. To say that I was nervous would not exactly describe the situation, and my condition was not improved by the keeper's parting whisper that his reputation was at stake as well as my own. Only one cock pheasant occupied that spinney, and he came over high and fast, to be crumpled up like a piece of paper. That night my father wrote to his favourite maker ordering a new breech-loader to be at once got in hand for me. I had arrived – after seven years tuition.'

An Old Un.

The Gamekeeper February 1920

Sons of Royalty

Even sons of royalty were taught to shoot by a head gamekeeper in times past. King George V, for example, listed as one of the fourth best shots in Great Britain by *Baily's* magazine in 1903, underwent a training programme during his youth devised by Charles Jackson, head keeper of the Sandringham estate, who was commanded by the Prince of Wales (later King Edward VII) to give him a thorough grounding in the art of safe gun handling and shooting.

If an adult took up shooting, he would be trained by the head gamekeeper, too, rather than by a proficient sportsman. Indeed, when former Prime Minister Harold Macmillan married Lady Dorothy Cavendish in 1920, his father-in-law, the 9th Duke of Devonshire, who expected him to participate in shoots at Chatsworth, arranged for Reg Roose, a gamekeeper, to teach him how to shoot correctly, even though he had never fired a shotgun in his life before.

Shooting continued to be taught in the time honoured manner on some large country estates until well into the late twentieth century. Indeed, Harry Grass,

Gamekeeper trained shot, King George V (on left), then Prince of Wales, shooting at Brocket Hall, Hertfordshire 1907

head gamekeeper to Earl Mountbatten of Burma at Broadlands in Hampshire, taught the earl's grandsons and a great nephew to shoot during the 1960s and '70s. Don Ford, head gamekeeper at Wimborne St.Giles in Dorset from 1974 until 1992, taught both the present Earl of Shaftesbury and his older brother how to shoot correctly. Even today, some of the more traditional sportsmen send their children out with a gamekeeper to pick-up 'hands on' skills to augment those that they have learned at a shooting school.

Gamekeeper shooting tuition was, however, very much the preserve of the aristocracy and the landed gentry in times past, and was not available to members of the general public who wished to learn to shoot. In fact, during the late Victorian period when game shooting was really starting to take off, newly rich businessmen, professionals and others who wanted to take up the sport were obliged to pick-up their gunnery skills from experienced friends or while serving in the Territorial Army.

Advertisement for Charles Lancaster's Private Shooting Grounds 1906

Private Shooting Schools

Keen to capitalise on the growing interest in game shooting, a number of well-known London gun makers opened private shooting grounds or schools within easy reach of the Metropolis to enable aspiring sportsmen to learn to shoot correctly and, just as importantly, to sample their products. Henry Holland established the Holland & Holland Shooting Ground in 1880, while Charles Lancaster opened his shooting ground at Stonebridge Park near Willesden Junction in the late 1880s. In 1901 Richard Watson set up the world famous West London Shooting School at Perivale (relocated to the present day site at Northolt in 1931).

Unlike gamekeeper tutors, who used live quarry for practice purposes, shooting schools trained their students using clay pigeon targets fired from a trap, a system invented by George Ligowsky of Ohio in 1880 and introduced into Great Britain shortly afterwards by Messrs Leobe & Co. Despite not being as testing as pheasants or partridges in the wild, clay pigeons (sometimes described as 'inanimate birds') nevertheless gave budding shots the opportunity to undertake simulated shooting in a variety of situations as well as to shoot at high bird targets released from towers.

Advertisement for clay pigeon shooting traps 1906

Clay pigeon shooting soon became popular as a sport, in addition to being used to train novice shots, as it enabled keen shots to go out shooting all year round if they so wished. The Inanimate Bird Shooting Association was formed for this purpose in 1892 and held the first clay pigeon shooting championship at Wimbledon in July, 1893. This organisation was succeeded by the Clay Pigeon Shooting Association (CPSA), founded in 1928, which continues to function at the present time.

Debonair Sportsmen

Some of the more debonair late Victorian and Edwardian sportsmen enrolled as students at London shooting schools, not so much as to improve their marksmanship or to shoot out of season, but in order to better their poise and to shoot in a stylish manner on the field. Many, though, continued to despise the use of clay pigeons for tuition purposes, considering gamekeeper training with live quarry in the countryside to be a more effective way of learning how to shoot correctly.

THE PUPIL OF A SHOOTING SCHOOL

'At present the aspiring sportsman of tender years is committed to the care of an instructor at a shooting school, and appears at a partridge drive or covert shoot fairly proficient as a shot and well drilled as to the careful handling of a gun. However, it is doubtful that he is superior in these matters to the youngster who has graduated at the hands of a keeper, and is certainly more lacking as regards other matters quite necessary to the education of a sportsman. The great advantage of learning to handle a gun at a shooting school is that the tyro does not wound and mangle lots of live game before acquiring proficiency, and it is one which will continue to tell in favour of the school as against the keeper's system of tuition, but inanimate is never the same as animate game, and the pupil at a school does not progress in woodcraft as he gains proficiency as a shot. This leads to a lot of young fellows being launched on a shooting field who spoil sport for themselves and often for others through ignorance of the habits of game.'

Clay Pigeon
The Gamekeeper July 1909

Gun (right) and valet-loader posing for the camera in a butt on a Yorkshire grouse moor 1934. During the 1920s and '30s valets, chauffeurs and other male servants who carried out loading duties were often trained at shooting schools

Shooting Schools in the 1920s and '30s

Shooting schools, however, really came into their own during the 1920s and '30s when it became the fashion for the young men of the day to be trained by a professional instructor rather than by a gamekeeper. Schools also started to provide loader tuition at this time, enabling valets, chauffeurs and other male servants who performed loading duties to learn how to handle a gun correctly. Lady shots, who were then something of a rarity, and generally were frowned upon both by sportsmen of long standing and members of the gamekeeping fraternity, invariably learned how to shoot properly at a school rather than on the family estate!

Tuition methods had now become quite sophisticated and many schools offered a variety of simulated shooting situations ranging from walked-up

Heap of spent cartridges at the Wembley Park Shooting Grounds 6 August 1931.
The caption on the back of the photograph reads: 'With the near approach of
"The Twelfth" shooting grounds are experiencing a busy time with
enthusiasts getting in practice before the opening of the season '

Learning to shoot the modern way: courtesy of the West London Shooting School

shooting through rough cover and 'rocketing pheasants' from a high hill to 'bolting rabbits', driven partridges over hedges and shooting from grouse butts. Some even boasted a selection of automatic traps and on-site gun fitting facilities. Shooting practice using clay pigeons was, of course, far more economical than shooting in the field, one hundred clay birds costing about the same as one head of game according to an advertisement placed in *Game & Gun* in 1937 by the West London Shooting Grounds.

World War Two

The various shooting schools were requisitioned by the authorities for military training purposes following the outbreak of World War Two in 1939. Aircraft gunners serving with RAF Bomber Command were given shooting tuition using clay pigeons at a number of schools together with anti-aircraft gun operators.

Students in action at the West London Shooting School: courtesy of the West London Shooting School

Schools were also used by the Army and the Royal Navy for specialist gunnery training activities.

Game bird rearing restrictions enacted by the Labour Government in the wake of World War Two gave shooting schools a renewed lease of life. In addition to offering tuition and practice, they were now able to provide clay pigeon shooting for experienced shots as a substitute for live birds, enabling those who were unable to access a pheasant or a partridge shoot due to game bird shortages to continue their shooting routine during the season.

Since this time, shooting schools have gone from strength to strength and today not only offer tuition for newcomers to the sport, be they young or old, but also provide out of season practice facilities for experienced shots and the opportunity for those who do not wish to kill live quarry to shoot inanimate targets in a safe environment. Schools have become more sophisticated over the years, embracing modern technology in the form of fully automated traps and using specially designed targets in the shape of rabbits, pheasants, snipe and other game rather than basic clay pigeons. Some schools offer laser clay pigeon shooting, too, using de-activated 12 bore shotguns, computer operated guidance systems and plastic clay targets activated by electronic traps.

THE
SUPPORT TEAM

SUCCESSFUL GAME SHOOTING relies upon an efficient support team, all of whom work hard in order to provide an enjoyable shooting day for their employer and his personal guests or paying Guns. The key players in the team are undoubtedly the gamekeeper and his staff and, where applicable, the professional shooting provider who sources and sells shooting and often acts as shoot captain, meeting and greeting clients upon their arrival at a shooting venue. Equally as important on the day itself are the beaters, the pickers-up, the loaders and the hostess who cooks and serves the meals at the shoot room or shooting lodge.

The gamekeeping staff on a Yorkshire estate c. 1910

The Gamekeeper

Shooting revolves around the activities of the gamekeeper, a talented and multi-skilled individual who gives selflessly of his time working long hours in all weathers to provide and protect his employer's game birds and ground game. His principal duties involve rearing, releasing and feeding game birds on low ground shoots; controlling avian and ground vermin humanely and legally; prevention of poaching; organising shooting days; and recruiting beaters, pickers-up and, in some cases, loaders. On a large estate, he will be in charge of the gun room and might be expected to breed and train gun dogs. He must be something of a diplomat, too, capable of communicating effectively and respectfully with sportsmen, farmers and other country folk, and members of the general public such as ramblers or dog walkers who traverse his preserves on footpaths or bridleways.

Group of gamekeepers c. 1860. Gamekeepers at this time were tough, no-nonsense men who regularly fought pitched battles with poachers

The gamekeeper has been a familiar figure in the countryside since the late seventeenth century. Initially he was employed to protect game birds from the predations of poachers, to maintain stocks of wild partridges and other quarry birds by trapping and snaring vermin and to attend gentlemen on the shooting field when game shooting was in its infancy. By the late Georgian period, he had become a skilled craftsman and had started to preserve pheasants and partridges for sporting purposes through nest management or by collecting and artificially incubating their eggs using broody hens.

Gamekeepers, however, remained fairly thin on the ground until the early nineteenth century, with few estates employing more than one or two keepers. Indeed as late as 1837 official statistics issued by the government estimated that the nation's gamekeeping force consisted of only around 8,000 men. This was at the time when shooting was really starting to become popular – in the wake of the Game Act of 1831 which removed the property qualification for killing game (enabling any purchaser of a Game Certificate to go out in pursuit of game on a farm or estate provided that he had the owner's permission to do so).

From the 1840s onwards, gamekeeping changed dramatically. The popularisation of driven game shooting, followed by the introduction of the breech-loading shotgun, which enabled a sportsman to kill a large number of game birds within a short space of time, suddenly created a demand for large stocks of pheasants and partridges and for gamekeepers who could produce and preserve them.

Landowners now started to recruit large teams of gamekeepers to artificially rear pheasants using broody hens, to preserve partridges through nest management and to bolster hare stocks by putting down imported live hares, in order that big bags of game could be shot on their properties. Head gamekeepers were appointed to take charge of game preservation on sporting estates; to allocate work to beat keepers who looked after a 'beat' or section of an estate; to train young men as additional keepers; and to liaise with other estate staff. Unlike other outdoor servants, who dealt with their master via a land agent, the head keeper usually had direct access.

William Kiddy, head gamekeeper at Withersfield, Suffolk, wearing a typical late Victorian keeper's outfit c. 1890

Throughout the late Victorian and Edwardian periods, a head gamekeeper on a large sporting property might be in charge of a staff of fifteen or more men, including beat keepers, under-keepers, woodmen, trappers, and, sometimes, a deer park keeper. Not only was he responsible for rearing tens of thousands of pheasants annually, he was empowered to dictate the cropping patterns on the tenant farms ensuring that they were in the best interests of game preservation. He was often in charge of forestry activities such as covert planting and ride

Gamekeepers employed by the 2nd Duke of Westminster on the Eaton estate in Cheshire c. late 1930s. Eaton was one of the few estates to maintain a large keepering staff during the inter-war years

widening. If head keeper on a grouse moor, he would invariably control the shepherds and regulate sheep stocks in order that grouse were given priority over sheep.

Gamekeeping as a profession reached its peak during the Edwardian era when driven game shooting dominated the field sports scene. Landowners competed with each other to provide their guests with daily bags of over 1,000 pheasants. During this period the number of gamekeepers employed on British estates increased from 17,000 men in 1900 to 23,000 in 1911. Shooting on a grand scale continued unabated until the outbreak of World War One in 1914.

Sadly, some of the gamekeepers who had survived the war were made redundant during the early 1920s as landowners started to cut back on shoot expenditure due to the effects of high taxation. It was not uncommon during the inter-war years for a gamekeeper on a small estate to combine his duties with farm or forestry work if a shoot was reduced in size or converted from driven to walked-up. By 1939, the number of gamekeepers employed in Great Britain had dropped to an estimated 10,000 men.

Shooting and gamekeeping suffered a further setback during World War Two after sporting estates were banned from rearing game birds and were ordered to cull stocks of pheasants and partridges to provide food for the war effort. Some keepers joined the armed forces for the duration while others served in the Home Guard – where their knowledge of firearms and fieldcraft skills stood them in good stead – or became full-time pest control officers at factories or munitions depots.

In the aftermath of World War Two, government-imposed game bird rearing restrictions, which remained in force until the mid-1950s, made it difficult for all but the wealthiest of landowners to rebuild a shoot.

Now a well-known countryside writer, Jill Mason became a gamekeeper in 1970 and spent over thirty years in the profession: courtesy of David Mason

Indeed, other than on very large estates, where a team of gamekeepers continued to be employed, most keepers now worked single-handedly, often carrying out various other duties ranging from gardening to acting as part-time chauffeur.

Since the 1960s, however, the interest in shooting has increased dramatically, fuelled by the growing demand for syndicate shooting and commercially let days, with the result that in the region of 3,000 men (and around one hundred women) continue to be employed as full-time gamekeepers in Great Britain at the present time. In addition, the various bodies which represent the shooting industry estimate that a similar number of men are currently involved in gamekeeping on a part-time basis, either assisting professional keepers during their spare time or through participation in small self-keepering shoots.

The gamekeeper of today can best be described as a 'countryside manager'. Unlike his predecessors who were trained 'on the job' in the game department

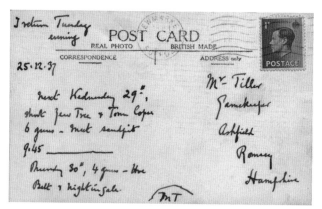

Postcard sent by Lord Mount Temple to his head gamekeeper, Bert Tiller advising him of forthcoming shooting engagements on the Broadlands estate in Hampshire 1937: courtesy of B. Whittle

of a country estate, he is likely to have spent some time learning his trade at a countryside college and will be fully conversant with game meat hygiene procedures, firearms regulations, wildlife and countryside legislation and public access matters in order that he can carry out his duties effectively. Indeed, for the past four decades or so education has played an important part in gamekeeper training. It must continue to do so in order for the profession of gamekeeping to survive the vicissitudes of the twenty-first century.

John Smith Grass – Edwardian Gamekeeper

John Smith Grass was born in 1865 on the Rufford Abbey estate in the Dukeries of Nottinghamshire, where his father, William Grass, was gamekeeper to Lord Saville, Queen Victoria's Ambassador to Italy. His story, based on interview by the author with his daughter, Kate, in 1983, provides a brief insight into the life of a gamekeeper on a great country estate in Edwardian England, often described as the era of the 'Big Shots', when driven game shooting was at its zenith and was the exclusive preserve of the elite.

Educated at the local village school, John began his gamekeeping career at the tender age of twelve in 1877, working alongside his father at Rufford Abbey. Having graduated from trainee keeper to under-keeper after he had learnt his trade, he eventually left Rufford in 1889 to join the Nottinghamshire Constabulary as a third-class police constable, based at Mansfield. He subsequently transferred to Eastwood and in 1890 was promoted to second-class constable

In 1891, finding life in the police force somewhat restrictive, John resigned from the Nottinghamshire Constabulary to become a beat keeper with Earl Cowper on the Beauvale estate near Greasley. Several years later he moved to Castle Donnington in Leicestershire to take a similar position with Lord Donnington. Unfortunately, following his lordship's death in 1895, he was dismissed along with the rest of the gamekeeping staff and was obliged to seek a new job elsewhere.

John soon secured employment as gamekeeper on the Sheriffhales Beat of the Lilleshall Hall estate on the Shropshire–Staffordshire border, one of several English sporting properties

John Smith Grass, gamekeeper and personal loader to the 4th Duke of Sutherland. Grass accompanied his employer to shoots throughout Great Britain and travelled to Dunrobin Castle in Sutherland with him every August to load on the grouse moors and to act as ghillie on the lochs and rivers

belonging to Cromartie, 4th Duke of Sutherland, who at that time ranked as the largest landowner in Western Europe. He joined a team of fourteen keepers, who, between them were responsible for game preservation in and around the villages of Lilleshall, Sheriffhales and Kynnersley. Each keeper was 6 foot 2 inches high, had the physique of a wrestler and possessed a faultless character – specifications demanded by the duke before he even considered interviewing a job applicant.

*Buck Gates Lodge, Thoresby Park, Nottinghamshire; a typical gamekeeper's lodge c. 1900.
It was not unusual for a keeper's wife to act as an unpaid gatekeeper and to open
and close the drive gates for carriages and motor cars*

The Duke of Sutherland paid his gamekeepers £1 a week and gave them a rent-free house, an unlimited supply of coal, and milk and butter from the home farm. Each man was provided with a pony and trap for his own use, a gun, an allowance of 1/6d. (7½ p) per week for each dog kept, and an annual payment of £3 in lieu of tips from shooting guests.

The gamekeepers usually dressed in a Sutherland homespun green tweed suit and matching cap made from tweeds woven on the duke's Scottish estates, a shirt and tie, cloth gaiters and leather boots. On shoot days they wore a ducal livery consisting of a special peaked cap, a green velvet coat with shining brass buttons bearing the Sutherland family crest, a green waistcoat, brown corduroy breeches, buckskin leggings and matching shoes.

John, his wife Eliza, and their young family quickly settled into 'Doublegates Lodge' which had been specially repaired and decorated for their occupation. John was now responsible for the Sheriffhales Beat which covered about 1,000 acres of the estate. Here, he was expected to rear 1,000 pheasants a year with occasional help, eliminate all vermin, prevent as much poaching as possible, and check that the tenant farmers were growing only crops which were conducive to game management.

Pheasants were reared traditionally. From April onwards John collected their eggs from nests in the woods and hedgerows and took them home to his rearing pens. He then placed them beneath tethered broody hens for incubation. Once hatched, the young chicks were fed on a mixture of maize, minced rabbit flesh, and mashed hard-boiled eggs, all cooked up in a huge copper. They remained with their 'foster mothers' until old enough to be taken to the rearing field – a small paddock surrounded by a high wire fence to keep out predators.

At the end of July, now poults, the young birds were taken to the woods to 'fill out' and await the start of the shooting season on 1 October. They still needed to be fed regularly in order to prevent them straying on to the Earl of Bradford's Weston Park estate which adjoined the beat. John's own special diet of grain and raisins sufficed for this purpose.

Although partridges, woodcock, snipe, hares and rabbits were all plentiful on the estate, pheasant shooting took pride of place over all other game bagged. On 6 January 1897, a typical Lilleshall shoot day, HRH the Prince of Wales, the Duke of Sutherland, the Marquess of Ormonde, the Earl of Dartmouth, Lord Herbert Vane-Tempest, Captain A. Halford, and W.H. Mildmay, Esq., between them shot 919 pheasants, 4 partridges, 67 hares and 70 rabbits.

Gamekeepers feeding young pheasants on a Sussex estate c. 1910

At the end of each shoot the game would be counted, logged in the estate game register, sorted into braces and taken back to the game larder at the Hall in the game cart – a specially made van drawn by two shire horses. Guests always received a brace or two of pheasants as a gift. Other birds were despatched by rail to Stafford House – the duke's London home, sent to a local hospital or sold to a game dealer. Rabbits and hares were distributed in pairs to outdoor staff such as lodge keepers, woodmen, labourers, or to the village sick.

If a shoot took place at Sheriffhales it was John's duty to take a brace of pheasants together with a hare or rabbit, to every tenant farmer on his beat. He would arrive home very late at night,

A Yorkshire gamekeeper with a display of dead vermin 1912

inebriated from the effects of the generous quantities of home-made wine or whisky given to him at each farmhouse. On one famous occasion, Dinah, his pony, returned home driverless, with him asleep in the back of the trap!

John only once missed one of these nocturnal outings. That was when the Duke of Sutherland's son, the Marquess of Stafford, accidentally shot him through the ear. Lord Stafford was so concerned about him that he ordered the duke's chauffeur to immediately drive John to the nearest railway station and put him on a train to London, where he was met and taken to a leading Harley Street ear specialist for treatment. Happily, both John and his ear survived with flying colours.

On non-shoot days John spent many hours shooting, trapping or laying strychnine baits to kill rats, squirrels, magpies, hawks and other vermin. In a hidden corner of a wood he had his 'sanctuary' where he hung out his quarry to dry on a line. This gory display was very necessary as he was paid a bounty of 1d for each creature present.

Dunrobin Castle in Sutherland, the Duke of Sutherland's Scottish shooting quarters

Poachers tended to avoid Lilleshall because the keepers had a reputation for being 'real terrors' to anyone they caught.

The Lilleshall gamekeepers were given one day's paid holiday a year. John was more fortunate than the others. As the Duke of Sutherland's personal loader he accompanied him to Scotland every August for the 'Glorious Twelfth'. They travelled north from Lilleshall to the fairytale Castle of Dunrobin at Golspie in Sutherland aboard a special train, complete with kennel and gun compartments, chartered from the London & North Western Railway Company. The party remained in Sutherland for a fortnight whilst the grouse shooting took place before returning to Shropshire for the start of the partridge shooting season on 1 September.

In 1902, John journeyed to Scotland twice. King Edward VII and Queen Alexandra visited Dunrobin aboard the Royal Yacht *Victoria and Albert*, in September of that year as shooting guests of the Sutherlands, prior to travelling by train to Balmoral for their annual holiday.

Cromartie, Duke of Sutherland, and Millicent, his Duchess, were model employers. At Lilleshall they operated a sick-pay scheme, provided a social club, regularly visited their employees' homes to check if improvements were needed, and sent gifts of tea and tobacco to local pensioners. Every Christmas the estate children visited the Hall to be given a present from the Christmas tree by the duchess. For the adults, there was the annual servants' ball hosted by their graces. If John was lucky he might manage to dance with Millicent, whilst his wife partnered Cromartie. When their son, Geordie, celebrated his twenty-first birthday in 1909, the villages on the estate were lavishly decorated with flags and bunting, a party was thrown for the employees, and an ox was roasted in the square at Newport, the nearest town to Lilleshall, with slices of meat being distributed amongst the needy of the district.

Life at Lilleshall looked set to continue for very many years, when, suddenly, in 1913, Cromartie died. He was succeeded as 5th Duke of Sutherland by his son, Geordie, who valiantly tried to save the estate despite massive death duties. Sadly, in 1917, he was forced to sell up. John was offered the opportunity to go with him to his new home, Sutton Place in Surrey, but declined, instead deciding to work for Benjamin James, a wealthy farmer who had purchased the Sheriffhales Beat. John remained as gamekeeper to Mr James until his retirement in 1937. He passed away in 1942 and was buried in the local cemetery. When his family returned home from his funeral they found that 'Sweep', his favourite retriever was missing. After hours of searching, his sons found the dog lying across his grave. This was quite a remarkable feat as 'Sweep' had never visited the cemetery before.

A whole way of life had vanished with the departure of the Dukes of Sutherland. Today most of the estate is in the hands of owner-occupiers whilst the Hall serves as the Lilleshall National Sports & Conferencing Centre.

The Beater

Employed to drive the game birds towards the Guns at a driven shoot, the beater has been an integral part of the support team on a shoot day since driven game shooting was introduced in the early nineteenth century. In times past, beaters were invariably estate workers who were redeployed from their day to day duties to assist on a shoot or local farm hands who were keen to augment their wages during late autumn and winter when other work was scarce. Beaters were originally known as 'brushers' in certain parts of Eastern England and as 'drivers' – a term still used on grouse shoots – in the northern counties and in Scotland.

Throughout the late Victorian and the Edwardian periods, it was not uncommon for between fifty to seventy beaters to be engaged on a large scale driven pheasant shoot. Beaters at this time were paid around 2/6d. (12½p) a day and were provided with a free lunch, which might consist of beer and sandwiches, baked potatoes and beer or hot stew and beer, dependent upon the generosity of the employer – some received a brace of rabbits to take home, too. On the more prestigious estates they were also supplied with protective clothing in the form of a white smock, a red hat and stout gaiters.

Shooting party at Brockworth, Gloucestershire c. 1900: courtesy of Eddy Graves, MBE. The gamekeepers and Guns are seated in the front row; the beaters are standing at the rear

Following the outbreak of World War One, many of the men who acted as beaters joined the armed forces, where they were to fight alongside gamekeepers and other countrymen. Beating work was subsequently carried out by elderly farm workers and land girls and in some instances German Prisoners of War, on estates where driven shoots still operated.

Throughout the inter-war years, beating on driven shoots continued to be undertaken by farm and estate staff, assisted in some cases by schoolboys or unemployed men recruited from a local Labour Exchange. Thereafter, the demand for beaters all but ceased when driven shooting was abandoned for the

Land girls (such as the young lady pictured above) regularly undertook beating duties during World War One

duration of World War Two. Large scale game shooting did not really start to take off again until the mid-1950s when a wartime ban on feeding game birds was lifted, enabling landowners to rebuild driven shoots.

Landowners subsequently encountered a 'beater shortage', caused by a decline in the rural population in many areas, a knock on effect of the agricultural mechanisation that had taken place in the immediate post-war period. Many now started to recruit suitable townsmen as well as countrymen to undertake beating duties, often providing an end of season beaters' shoot to encourage regular attendance on shoot days.

Beating has gradually changed beyond all recognition over the past half century or so and has become something of a social occasion rather than an opportunity for a farm worker to earn extra money to supplement low agricultural wages. Indeed a modern beating team might easily include a car mechanic, a bank manager and a prosperous businessman, as well as two or three women, all of whom can shoot just as well as any of the Guns on the shooting field.

Beating on a driven game shoot is more popular than ever before, attracting men and women from all walks of life, even though remuneration is relatively modest, perhaps £25 to £40 a day with a cooked lunch and a couple of brace of pheasants or partridges to take home. Beaters now have their own professional body, the National Organisation of Beaters and Pickers Up (founded in 2005 and commonly known as NOBS), which acts as an agency to provide beaters for shoots and represents their interests in countryside matters.

Writing in 1934, Archibald Weyland Ruggles-Brise gives some advice regarding the deployment of beaters on the shooting field:

'In driving coverts the beaters should walk slowly, and beat every bush, and should not be asked to shirk the thick bushes. If there are a lot of brambles and thorn bushes to encounter, it will make the day go better for all concerned if every beater is provided with a smock, which is handed back to the keeper at the end of the day. A good luncheon and a glass of beer makes all the difference to the beaters. Each beater should be provided with a meat and cheese sandwich, so that all are equally served. In the olden days a large tin of stew was brought out, and each helped himself. The result was that the beaters who were keen and helped to pick up the game after a drive, arrived for luncheon and found, as in Mother Hubbard's cupboard, "the stewpot bare".'

The Picker-Up

Originally known as a 'dog man', the picker-up or dog handler has been an integral part of the beating team on a driven shoot since the Victorian period. Employed to pick-up dead or wounded game at the end of each drive using a specially trained dog, he or she enjoys the same remuneration as a beater, but tends to be paid slightly more and can earn up to £70 per day. In times past, picking-up duties were carried out by gamekeepers from nearby estates, but, since the late 1940s, have generally been undertaken by 'specialist' dog handlers, often ladies, who usually own several gun dogs.

Picker-up in action: courtesy of the GWCT

The Loader

One of the most important team members on a driven shoot, the loader not only replenishes a sportsman's guns with cartridges as quickly as possible to allow him to shoot at game birds continuously but is also responsible for cleaning them and for their security. He is invariably an extremely knowledgeable individual who can, if necessary, act as a mentor to a young or inexperienced shot, advising him or her on safe shooting procedures, quarry identification, shoot etiquette and general countryside matters.

The first loaders, however, were little more than personal attendants who accompanied sportsmen when out walked-up shooting in order to carry the necessary material and equipment to charge a muzzle-loading shotgun. Usually a gamekeeper or a household manservant, these attendants also acted as beater. They carried their master's food and kept a large flask of brandy in a coat pocket for use as a restorative in the event of a shooting accident caused by damp powder or a badly filled gun, or as a general 'pick-me-up'.

Edwardian sportsman pheasant shooting with his loader standing behind

Loader-attendants were replaced by dedicated loaders following the introduction of the breech-loading shotgun in the mid-nineteenth century, which enabled a sportsman to kill a large bag of game birds within a short space of time using double guns. Competent, sober men who could load and change guns with precision and style were selected for this role. Some loaders were even chosen because they were of a similar height and stature to their masters and were supplied with an identical tweed suit and hat to wear on shoot days so that both men were of fashionable appearance.

Sportsmen usually recruited loaders on an 'in house' basis, either from the household or the estate staff, the most popular candidates being a valet or an under-keeper, although it was not unknown for a suitable gardener or farm labourer to be asked to load. Often a young, single man, he was expected to travel with his master wherever he went shooting, be it on his own estate or as an invited guest either at home or abroad. Those selected to act as loaders would, of course, if not from a gamekeeping background, receive appropriate training from the estate's head gamekeeper.

Loader (on left) and sportsman changing guns on a Hampshire shoot 1975:
courtesy of the GWCT

Loading continued to be carried out in the time honoured manner by gamekeepers and other servants until the 1970s, although by this time double gun shooting was something of a rarity apart from on the more prestigious estates or grouse moors. Thereafter, shoot owners, especially those operating commercial shoots, began to provide their own loaders for health and safety reasons, in order to have experienced men with an in-depth knowledge of the shooting field layout and to enable repeat clients to have their own regular loader, if required. Like beating, loading started to attract men and women from all walks of life and today loaders can range from retired gamekeepers, self-employed countryside craftsmen and 'lady loaders' who might earn from £50 to £100 a day, to professional men who load every Saturday in return for a couple of day's boundary shooting and an invitation to the end of season beaters' shoot.

Over the past decade or so, a number of sport-related organisations have introduced loader training courses, enabling aspiring loaders and experienced professionals such as gamekeepers, personal servants and country estate staff to become aware of relevant health and safety procedures, loading techniques, double gunning procedures, shooting etiquette and other related issues.

Professional Shooting Providers

The professional shooting provider acts as an intermediary between a sportsman who wishes to purchase a day's shooting, and a landowner, a shooting syndicate, a shoot manager or other shoot operator who sells shooting on a commercial or semi-commercial basis. He charges a commission fee for his services and can usually arrange overnight accommodation for clients, vehicle hire and other facilities, if required. Shooting providers range from specialist sporting agents and rural estate agencies with a letting department to shoot managers, gunsmiths, hoteliers and shoot owners themselves.

The Sporting Agent

Essentially a full-time professional shooting provider, the sporting agent sources and sells shooting, fishing and deer stalking to British and foreign clients either on a daily basis or in the form of a residential package for a fixed period of time. Some agents also operate 'roving' or 'roaming' syndicates which enable clients to shoot on a variety of different estates or grouse moors and act as agents for overseas shooting or safari companies in Spain, Mexico, Eastern Europe, Africa and other parts of the world.

Sporting agency began in a small way during the early Victorian period when gun smiths, solicitors, estate agents and others involved with shooting or land management started to advertise and sell sporting rights over estates or large farms to well-off businessmen, members of the professional classes or men of independent means living in towns and cities who were keen to have a shoot of their own. The first full-time professional sporting agents, although based in London, were involved primarily with the Scottish sporting letting industry, leasing or renting grouse moors, deer forests and salmon fishings to wealthy clients on behalf of landowners north of the Border. James Watson Lyall, for

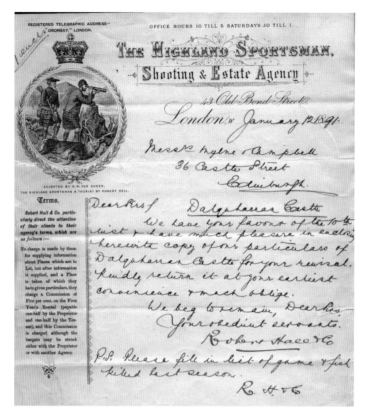

Letter sent to a client by Robert Hall & Co., proprietors of the Highland Sportsman Shooting and Estate agency, one of a number of London based agents which specialised in letting Scottish sporting properties 1891

example, editor and proprietor of *The Sportsman's and Tourist's Guide to the Timetables, Rivers, Moors and Deer Forests of Scotland* (an annual publication for sportsmen visiting Scotland) opened The Sportsman's Guide, Shooting and Fishing Agency at 15, Pall Mall in 1879. Within a few years, he confidently told members of the sporting fraternity that he offered 'the largest selection of Scotch shootings to let which can be found anywhere'.

In addition to offering shootings and fishings in Scotland, London sporting agents began to sell elk and ryper shooting rights in Norway, salmon fishing in Iceland and big game hunting in parts of Africa and Asia. Messrs Lumley & Dowell of St. James's Street was founded in the late 1890s and was obviously one of the more adventurous agencies advertising 'Scandinavian elk, reindeer, red deer and ryper shooting' and offering to arrange seal clubbing in the Outer Hebrides, shooting in Canada and fishing in Norway. They were even able to charter whaling ships for private sporting expeditions.

The letting of sporting rights over English, Welsh and Irish estates, however, continued to be largely handled by solicitors, surveyors, gunsmiths and other part-time agents until the mid-twentieth century when the ever increasing demand for shooting and fishing on a daily or a weekly basis made it viable for sporting enthusiasts to set up specialist sporting agencies. Curtis & Henson of London, one of the first of such agencies, founded by Cecil Fielden, Jeremy Wilson and Francis Holdsworth Hunt in the late 1940s, later acquired the Captain Percy Wallace Agency (successors of James Watson Lyall's Sportsman's Guide, Shooting and Fishing Agency) and in the 1980s became a part of Roxtons of Hungerford, currently one of Britain's leading agencies which offer clients a global sporting portfolio.

Over the past forty years or so, sporting agency has become big business, fuelled partly by the growth in commercial shooting. Specialist sporting agents can now be found in many parts of the country and can often arrange shooting and fishing both at home and abroad. Some gun makers, estate agents and large shoot owners operate 'in house' sporting agencies, too. Sporting agency has also gone online within the past decade in the form of the GunsOnPegs website, a free-to-use site set up by entrepreneur and keen shot, James Horne, which enables members and shoot owners to buy and sell shooting via the internet.

The Shoot Manager

Something of a newcomer to the world of game shooting, the shoot manager first began to appear in the 1970s and has become increasingly common. Often a former gamekeeper, he rents or leases the sporting rights on an estate (usually doing his own gamekeeping) and operates a shoot on a commercial basis, letting out pheasant and partridge shooting to paying Guns. Some large sporting estates employ an 'in house' shoot manager, either to run a commercial shoot or simply to let and oversee shoot days.

Sporting Letting

Sporting letting undoubtedly dates back to the late Georgian period when English landowners began to rent out country estates either for financial reasons or because they were surplus to requirements, to suitably qualified tenants. For example, the Drummond family leased The Grange estate at Alresford in Hampshire to the Prince Regent for use as a shooting and hunting box. Scottish lairds followed suit, letting out grouse moors, salmon fishings, deer stalking and lodge accommodation to wealthy sportsmen from south of the Border for the summer months each year. Letting transactions at this time were often of an informal nature, with trivial amounts of money being paid for some Scottish shootings.

Letting prospectus for the Hafod Shootings in Cardiganshire 1868

The practice of letting out shootings and fishings on a proper business footing, however, did not really start until the late 1830s when landowners realised that they could make sizeable sums of money by renting out sporting rights over their properties to newly rich but landless industrialists and professional men who were prepared to pay handsomely for the privilege of shooting over a country estate, particularly if it was near to a town or a city or within reasonable proximity of a railway station. Often using a gun maker, a solicitor or other intermediary to act as a sporting agent, some members of the English and Welsh landed gentry began to rent out or to lease the shootings over outlying portions of their estate to sporting tenants, either annually or for a fixed term of years. In Scotland and Ireland, whole estates were marketed in this way, with landowners putting their own house at the tenant's disposal for use as shooting quarters during summer and autumn. By the mid-nineteenth century, sporting letting had become a boom industry with one agent, alone, Hugh Snowie (an Inverness gun maker) claiming to have around 150 Scottish sporting properties on his books.

Many of the more astute landowners of the day started to draw up legally binding rental agreements using a solicitor or a land agent in order to ensure that their property was not over-shot or over-fished, and to protect the interests of their farming tenants. Such agreements usually imposed strict bag limits for game conservation reasons, required that returns of all game shot should be submitted annually, prohibited subletting to a third party and stipulated that if a sporting tenant employed his own gamekeeper, the gamekeeper should also be accountable to the estate head gamekeeper.

Scottish and Irish landowners did very well financially out of sporting letting from the mid-Victorian period until 1914, building luxurious shooting lodges to accommodate wealthy tenants and improving the shooting, fishing and deer stalking facilities on their properties. Some of their English and Welsh counterparts profited, too, especially those who let out grouse moors to members of the aristocracy, rich businessmen or American sportsmen who made an annual pilgrimage to Great Britain by liner in order to shoot grouse.

Shooting on many let estates was disbanded for the duration of the war, either because the estate had been requisitioned for military purposes or because the tenant had enlisted in the armed services or was prohibited from visiting the property due to travel restrictions. Thereafter, from the end of World War One until 1939, sporting letting, in many cases, simply became a means to an end. It enabled an impecunious landowner hit by high taxation or death duties to let out his entire estate complete with a country house and shooting and fishing rights, to a wealthy peer or businessman, a shooting syndicate or an adjoining shoot owner for a fixed term of years in order to pay off accrued debts and to preserve the estate for future generations.

LEASING AN ENGLISH SHOOT – 1930s STYLE

Lord Davies of Llandinam, a Welsh politician and railway magnate, leased Tendring Hall at Stoke-by-Nayland in Suffolk together with the shooting rights over 3,105 acres of land from Sir Joshua Rowley, Bt., for a term of seven years from April 1931 until April 1938 at a rental of £1,100 per annum. A keen shot and angler, he was responsible for paying the following estate outgoings on top of his yearly rental fee:

1) Retain at least four gamekeepers, pay their wages, buy their gun and game licences and provide them with livery uniforms.

2) Pay the wages of the head gardener and under-gardeners.

3) Provide the food for the young game birds, and pay any other expenses connected with the preservation of game.

4) Pay rent for any ground required outside the woods and coverts for rearing game, other than for a rearing ground not exceeding ten acre in extent on the Home Beat.

5) Pay the cost of annually fencing in the rearing ground with hurdles.

6) Pay any necessary compensation to tenant farmers on the estate for damage caused by game birds and rabbits.

7) Pay for the destruction of rabbits in the various coverts and in the park, otherwise the proprietor would have the right to enter these grounds between 1 January and 1 April in any year and remove the rabbits with nets and ferrets and sell them for his own benefit.

8) Pay for the winding of outside clocks on estate buildings.

In addition to paying all of these expenses, Lord Davies was expected to 'Exercise the right of sporting in a sportsmanlike manner, to keep up the head of game on the estate and to the best of his power preserve the eggs and young of game birds from being destroyed or injured.'

THE NATIONAL TRUST has the Shoot on its Holnicote Estate (between Porlock and Minehead, Somerset) to let for the 1958 season and longer if desired. The Shoot covers an area of some 10,000 acres of land, of which about 4,000 acres comprise a good, rough Pheasant Shoot with some well placed coverts offering fine stands. This Estate has been one of the best wild bird shoots in the West Country and has produced strong stock over many years. The remainder consists of that part of Exmoor near Dunkery Beacon on which there are Grouse and Woodcock. The services of the present keeper could be retained.—Applications should be made to: The Area Agent, The National Trust, Holnicote Estate Office, nr. Minehead, Somerset.

Letting advertisement for the National Trust owned Holnicote Shoot in Somerset 1958

Since the end of World War Two sporting letting has changed considerably. Many estates have been reduced in size, with the farms and their attendant sporting rights being sold to the tenants, often on a haphazard basis, making it less viable for a landowner to lease the shootings over a large tract of land to a private individual or a syndicate. In fact, today, it is not uncommon for a group of neighbouring landowners and farmers to let out the shooting rights over their respective properties to a commercial shoot operator in order that he can run a driven shoot over a sizeable area. Letting, itself, is now generally carried out using a specialist sporting agent or an estate agency or, exceptionally, directly between a landowner and a client.

Bibliography, Further Reading, References and Sources

Alington, Charles: *Partridge Driving*; John Murray Ltd, 1904
Alken, Henry: *The National Sports of Great Britain*, 1821

Bacon, Peter: *Land, Lust & Gun Smoke – A Social History of Game Shoots In Ireland*; The History Press Ireland, 2012
Beaven, T.P.: *A Sportsman Looks Back*; B. Lansdown & Sons Ltd, 1938
Billett, Michael: *A History of English Country Sports*; Robert Hale Ltd, 1994
Boynton, Lady Mildred: *Ladies in the Field*, 1894
Braithwaite, Cecil: *Fishing Vignettes*; Home Words Ltd, 1923
Brander, Michael: *Hunting & Shooting: From Earliest Times to the Present Day*; Weidenfeld & Nicolson, 1971

Denys, Bt., Sir Francis: *Sporting Journal*; unpublished manuscript
Dorchester, Lord: *Sport: Foxhunting and Shooting*; Rich & Cowan Ltd, 1935

Everitt, Nicholas and Watson, Dr E.I.: *Shots from a Lawyer's Gun*; Gilbertson & Page, 1927

Field, The: various articles, 1858 and 1868
Fitzgerald, Gerald: *Pot Luck: Rough Shooting in The West of Ireland*; Herbert Jenkins Ltd, 1938
Freeman, Captain W.: *The Pheasant from the Cradle to the Grave*; Alfred R. Knapp, 1900

Gamekeeper, The: 1897–1940
Gladstone, Sir Hugh S.: *Record Bags and Shooting Records*; The Signet Press, 1995
Gordon, Lord Granville: *Sporting Reminiscences*; Grant Richards, 1902
Greville, Lady Violet (editor): *Ladies in the Field: Sketches of Sport*; D. Appleton & Co., 1894

Hanger, Colonel George: *Advice to all Sportsmen, Farmers and Gamekeepers*, 1814
Harrison, CB, CBE, MC, Major-General Eric: *Gunners, Game & Gardens*; Leo Cooper, 1978
Hartopp, Colonel E.C.C.: *Sport in England: Past and Present*; The Field Office, 1894
Hawker, Colonel Peter: *The Diary of Colonel Peter Hawker 1802–1853*; Longmans, Green & Co., 1893
Hill, Shelagh: *Early Memories of Settlers in Machakos, Kenya*; published privately, 2005
Hipgrave, Arthur: *The Management of a Partridge Beat*; Arthur L. Humphreys, 1922
Hobson, J.C. Jeremy and Jones, David S.D.: *Sporting Lodges: Sanctuaries, Havens and Retreats*; Quiller, 2013

'Idstone': *The Idstone Papers*; The Field Office, 1874

Jones, David S.D.: *Harry Grass – King of the Gamekeepers*; published privately, 2011
Jones, David S.D.: *Gamekeeping: An Illustrated History*; Quiller, 2014
Jones, David S.D.: The David S.D. Jones Gamekeeping Archive and Photographic Collection

Kirby, David: *Country House Scenes in North Yorkshire in the Nineteenth Century*; published privately for Sir Anthony Milbank, Bt., 2007

Lloyd-Price, R.J.: *Rabbits for Profit and Rabbits for Powder*; Horace Cox, 1888

Martelli, George: *The Elveden Enterprise*; Faber & Faber Ltd, 1952
Maxwell, Captain Aymer: *Partridges and Partridge Manors*; Adam & Charles Black, 1911
Maxwell, W.H.: *Wild Sports of The West*; The Talbot Press Ltd, no date but probably 1930s
McDougall, Keith: *A Special Kind of Light: Norfolk and Scottish Landscapes*; Roseworld, 2009
McLean, Colin: *At Dawn and Dusk*; The Batchworth Press, 1954

Nickerson, Sir Joseph: *A Shooting Man's Creed*; Sidgwick & Jackson Ltd, 1989

Oakleigh, Thomas: *The Shooting Code*; 1836

Payne-Gallwey, Sir Ralph: *Letters to Young Shooters*; Longmans, Green & Co., 1894
Pennell-Elmhirst, Captain Edward: *Foxhound, Forest and Prairie*; George Routledge & Sons Ltd, 1892
Portland, KG, KCVO, 6th Duke of: *Men Women and Things*; Faber & Faber Ltd, 1938
Prichard, H. Hesketh: *Hunting Camps in Wood and Wilderness*; Thomas Nelson & Sons, 1910

Rose, Georgina: *A Countrywoman's Year*; Barrie & Jenkins Ltd, 1973
Ruffer, Jonathan Garnier: *The Big Shots*; Debrett's Peerage Ltd, 1977
Ruggles-Brise, Archibald Weyland: *Shooting Reminiscences in Essex and Elsewhere*; published privately, 1936

Stanfield, F.G.: *Pheasant Shooting*; Percival Marshall & Co., 1963
Stephens, Martin: *Grouse Shooting*; Adam & Charles Black, 1939
'Stonehenge': *Manual of British Rural Sports*; Routledge, Warnes & Routledge, 1859

Teasdale-Buckell, G.T.: *The Complete Shot*; Methuen & Co. Ltd, 1907
Thomas, B.: *The Shooter's Guide*, 1820
Thornhill, R.B.: *Sporting Directory*, 1804
Turner, T.W.: *Memoirs of a Gamekeeper*; Geoffrey Bles, 1954

Wade, Henling Thomas: *With Boat and Gun in the Yangtze Valley*; Shanghai Mercury Ltd, 1910
Walsingham, Lord and Payne-Gallwey, Sir Ralph: *The Badminton Library: Shooting in Field and Covert*; Longmans, Green & Co., 1886
Walsingham, Lord and Payne-Gallwey, Sir Ralph: *The Badminton Library: Shooting in Moor and Marsh*; Longmans, Green & Co., 1887
Watson, Alfred E.T.: *English Sport*; Macmillan & Co. Ltd, 1903

Index

Page numbers in *italic* refer to captions